T0354750

GENE RATI ONS

ANNETTE FLUKER

authorHOUSE®

AuthorHouse™
1663 Liberty Drive
Bloomington, IN 47403
www.authorhouse.com
Phone: 1 (800) 839-8640

Published by AuthorHouse 11/08/2018

ISBN: 978-1-5462-6779-9 (sc)
ISBN: 978-1-5462-6778-2 (e)

Print information available on the last page.

Any people depicted in stock imagery provided by Getty Images are models,
and such images are being used for illustrative purposes only.
Certain stock imagery © Getty Images.

This book is printed on acid-free paper.

Because of the dynamic nature of the Internet, any web addresses or
links contained in this book may have changed since publication and
may no longer be valid. The views expressed in this work are solely those
of the author and do not necessarily reflect the views of the publisher,
and the publisher hereby disclaims any responsibility for them.

Scripture quotations marked NIV are taken from the Holy
Bible, New International Version®. NIV®. Copyright ©
1973, 1978, 1984 by International Bible Society. Used by
permission of Zondervan. All rights reserved. [Biblica]

Then god said let us make mankind in our own image, in our likeness, so that they may rule

Over the fish in the sea and the birds in the sky, over the livestock and all the wild animals and over the creature's that move along the ground. So god created mankind in his own image.

In the image of god he created them male and female. God blessed them and said be fruitful, these humans god made, adam and eve, adam from dust of the ground and breathed in his nostrils the breath of life and the man became a living being, the great creatures of the sea, every living thing with which the water teams and that moves

Israel by violating the ban on taking devoted things.

The son of ethan;
Azariah
The sons born to hezron were;
Jerahmeel, ram and caleb.
From ram son to hezron
Ram was the father of
Amminadab, and amminadab the father of nahshon, the leader, of the people of judah.
Nahshon was the father of salmon, salmon the father of boaz
Boaz the father of obed and obed the father of jesse .
Jesse was the father of eliab his firstborn ; the second son was abinadab ,the third shimea, the fourth nethanel the fifth raddai, the sixth ozem and the seventh david.
Their sisters were zeruiah and abigail. zeruiah and abigil. zeruiahs three sons were abishai, joab, and asahel.
Abigail was the mother of amasa whose father was jether the ishaelite.
Caleb son of hezron

the fatherjair

about it according to its kind . the livestock the creatures that move along the ground.

Adam and eve the parents of cain also abel,cain killed abel,cain soon got a wife and had a son enoch, enoch had a son irad, irad was the father of mehujael and mehujael was the father of methushael, and methushael was the father of lamaech.

Lamaech married two women, one name was adah and the other zillah .adah gave birth to jabel,he was the father of those who lived in tents and raised livestock

His brother name was jubal, he was the father of all who played stringed instruments and pipes.

Israel by violating the ban on taking devoted things.

The son of ethan;
Azariah
The sons born to hezron were;
Jerahmeel, ram and caleb.
From ram son to hezron
Ram was the father of
Amminadab, and amminadab the father of nahshon, the leader, of the people of judah.
Nahshon was the father of salmon, salmon the father of boaz
Boaz the father of obed and obed the father of jesse .
Jesse was the father of eliab his firstborn ; the second son was abinadab ,the third shimea, the fourth nethanel the fifth raddai, the sixth ozem and the seventh david.
Their sisters were zeruiah and abigail. zeruiah and abigil. zeruiahs three sons were abishai, joab, and asahel.
Abigail was the mother of amasa whose father was jether the ishaelite.
Caleb son of hezron

the fatherjair

Zillah also had a son tubal-cain who forged all kinds of tools out of bronze and iron, tubal-cain sister was naamah.

Adam made love to his wife again,and she gave birth to a son seth.

Seth had a son and named him enoch

At this time people began to call on the lord.

God created mankind he made them in the likeness of god.

He created them male and female and blessed them, and he made them mankind when they were created.

Israel by violating the ban on taking devoted things.

The son of ethan;
Azariah
The sons born to hezron were;
Jerahmeel, ram and caleb.
From ram son to hezron
Ram was the father of
Amminadab, and amminadab the father of nahshon, the leader, of the people of judah.
Nahshon was the father of salmon, salmon the father of boaz
Boaz the father of obed and obed the father of jesse .
Jesse was the father of eliab his firstborn ; the second son was abinadab ,the third shimea, the fourth nethanel the fifth raddai, the sixth ozem and the seventh david.
Their sisters were zeruiah and abigail. zeruiah and abigil. zeruiahs three sons were abishai, joab, and asahel.
Abigail was the mother of amasa whose father was jether the ishaelite.
Caleb son of hezron

the fatherjair

When adam had lived 130 years, he had a son in his own likeness,in his own likeness

In his own image and he named him seth, after seth was born adam lived 800 years and other sons daughters altogether adam lived a total of 930 years and he died. When seth lived 105 year's he became the father of enoch. After he became the father of enoch seth lived 807 years and had other sons and daughters altogether seth lived a total 912 years and then he died.

When enoch had lived 90 years he became the father of kenan after he became the father of kenan,enoch lived 815 years and had other son's and daughters, all together enoch lived a total of 905 years and then he died.

Israel by violating the ban on taking devoted things.

The son of ethan;
Azariah
The sons born to hezron were;
Jerahmeel, ram and caleb.
From ram son to hezron
Ram was the father of
Amminadab, and amminadab the father of nahshon, the leader, of the people of judah.
Nahshon was the father of salmon, salmon the father of boaz
Boaz the father of obed and obed the father of jesse .
Jesse was the father of eliab his firstborn ; the second son was abinadab ,the third shimea, the fourth nethanel the fifth raddai, the sixth ozem and the seventh david.
Their sisters were zeruiah and abigail. zeruiah and abigil. zeruiahs three sons were abishai, joab, and asahel.
Abigail was the mother of amasa whose father was jether the ishaelite.
Caleb son of hezron

the fatherjair

When kenan had lived 70 years he became the father of mahalalel

After he became the father of mahalalel kenan lived 840 years and had other son's and daughters altogether kenan lived 910 years and then he died.

When mahalalel lived a total of 895 years and then he died, when jared had lived 162 years he became the father of enoch, after he became the father of enoch jared lived 800 years and had other sons and daughters altogether jared lived a total of 962 years and then he died.

When enoch lived 65 years he became the father of methuselah, after he became the father of methuselah enoch walked faithfully with god 300 years and had other

---

Israel by violating the ban on taking devoted things.

The son of ethan;
Azariah
The sons born to hezron were;
Jerahmeel, ram and caleb.
From ram son to hezron
Ram was the father of
Amminadab, and amminadab the father of nahshon, the leader, of the people of judah.
Nahshon was the father of salmon, salmon the father of boaz
Boaz the father of obed and obed the father of jesse .
Jesse was the father of eliab his firstborn ; the second son was abinadab ,the third shimea, the fourth nethanel the fifth raddai, the sixth ozem and the seventh david.
Their sisters were zeruiah and abigail. zeruiah and abigil. zeruiahs three sons were abishai, joab, and asahel.
Abigail was the mother of amasa whose father was jether the ishaelite.
Caleb son of hezron

the fatherjair

sons and daughters altogether enoch lived 365 year's . enoch walked faithfully with god then he was no more because god took him away.

When methuselah had lived 187 years he became the father of lamech methuselah lived 782 years and had other sons and daughters.

Altogether methuselah lived a total of 969 years and then he died, when lamech had lived 182 years he had a son he named him noah and he said he will comfort us.

Lamech lived 595 years and had other sons and daughters,altogether lamech lived a total of 777 years then he died. after noah was 500 years old he became

Israel by violating the ban on taking devoted things.

The son of ethan;
Azariah
The sons born to hezron were;
Jerahmeel, ram and caleb.
From ram son to hezron
Ram was the father of
Amminadab, and amminadab the father of nahshon, the leader, of the people of judah.
Nahshon was the father of salmon, salmon the father of boaz
Boaz the father of obed and obed the father of jesse .
Jesse was the father of eliab his firstborn ; the second son was abinadab ,the third shimea, the fourth nethanel the fifth raddai, the sixth ozem and the seventh david.
Their sisters were zeruiah and abigail. zeruiah and abigil. zeruiahs three sons were abishai, joab, and asahel.
Abigail was the mother of amasa whose father was jether the ishaelite.
Caleb son of hezron

the fatherjair

the father of shem, ham, japheth, when humans began to increase in numbers.

When humans begin to increase in numbers on the earth and daughters were born to them the sons of god saw that the daughters of humans were beautiful and they married any of them they chose. Then the lord said my spirit will not contend with humans forever for they are mortal their days will be one hundred and twenty years, the nephilim were on the earth in those days, when lamech lived 182 years he had a son,he named him noah and said he will comfort us in the labor and painful toil of our hands caused by the ground the lord has cursed.

Israel by violating the ban on taking devoted things.

The son of ethan;
Azariah
The sons born to hezron were;
Jerahmeel, ram and caleb.
From ram son to hezron
Ram was the father of
Amminadab, and amminadab the father of nahshon, the leader, of the people of judah.
Nahshon was the father of salmon, salmon the father of boaz
Boaz the father of obed and obed the father of jesse .
Jesse was the father of eliab his firstborn ; the second son was abinadab ,the third shimea, the fourth nethanel the fifth raddai, the sixth ozem and the seventh david.
Their sisters were zeruiah and abigail. zeruiah and abigil. zeruiahs three sons were abishai, joab, and asahel.
Abigail was the mother of amasa whose father was jether the ishaelite.
Caleb son of hezron

the fatherjair

When the sons of god went to the daughters of humans and had children by them,they were the heroes of old men of renown.

The lord saw how great the wickedness of the human race had become on earth and that every inclination of the thoughts of the humans heart was evil all the time, the lord regretted that he had made human being on earth, and his heart was deeply troubled, so the lord said, i will wipe from the face of earth the human race i created and with them the animals, the birds and the creatures that move along the ground, for i regret that i have made them, but noah found favor in the eyes of the lord.

Israel by violating the ban on taking devoted things.

The son of ethan;
Azariah
The sons born to hezron were;
Jerahmeel, ram and caleb.
From ram son to hezron
Ram was the father of
Amminadab, and amminadab the father of nahshon, the leader, of the people of judah.
Nahshon was the father of salmon, salmon the father of boaz
Boaz the father of obed and obed the father of jesse .
Jesse was the father of eliab his firstborn ; the second son was abinadab ,the third shimea, the fourth nethanel the fifth raddai, the sixth ozem and the seventh david.
Their sisters were zeruiah and abigail. zeruiah and abigil. zeruiahs three sons were abishai, joab, and asahel.
Abigail was the mother of amasa whose father was jether the ishaelite.
Caleb son of hezron

the fatherjair

Noah was a righteous man blameless among the people of his time, and he walked faithfully with god, noah had three sons shem, ham, and japheth.

Now the earth was corrupt in god's sight and was full of violence.

God saw how corrupt the earth had become for all the people on earth had corrupted their ways, so god said to noah, i'm going to put and end to all the people for the earth is full of violence because of them.

Iam surely going to destroy both them and the earth, so make yourself an ark of cypress wood . i am going to bring floodwaters on the earth to destroy all life under the heavens every creature that has the breath of life in

---

Israel by violating the ban on taking devoted things.

The son of ethan;
Azariah
The sons born to hezron were;
Jerahmeel, ram and caleb.
From ram son to hezron
Ram was the father of
Amminadab, and amminadab the father of nahshon, the leader, of the people of judah.
Nahshon was the father of salmon, salmon the father of boaz
Boaz the father of obed and obed the father of jesse .
Jesse was the father of eliab his firstborn ; the second son was abinadab ,the third shimea, the fourth nethanel the fifth raddai, the sixth ozem and the seventh david.
Their sisters were zeruiah and abigail. zeruiah and abigil. zeruiahs three sons were abishai, joab, and asahel.
Abigail was the mother of amasa whose father was jether the ishaelite.
Caleb son of hezron

the fatherjair

it . everything on earth will perish. Enter the ark you and your sons and your wife and your sons wives with you. Never again will all life be destroyed by the waters of a flood,never again will there be a flood to destroy the earth,and god said,this is the sign of the covenant i am making between me and you and every living creature with you, a covenant for all generations to come. I have set my rainbow in the clouds and it will be the sign of the covenant between me and the living earth, whenever i bring clouds over the earth and the rainbows appears in the clouds, i will see it and remember the everlasting between god and all, the everlasting covenant between god and all living creatures of every kind on the earth .so god said to noah,this is the sign of the covenant,i have established between me and all life on the earth.

Israel by violating the ban on taking devoted things.

The son of ethan;
Azariah
The sons born to hezron were;
Jerahmeel, ram and caleb.
From ram son to hezron
Ram was the father of
Amminadab, and amminadab the father of nahshon, the leader, of the people of judah.
Nahshon was the father of salmon, salmon the father of boaz
Boaz the father of obed and obed the father of jesse .
Jesse was the father of eliab his firstborn ; the second son was abinadab ,the third shimea, the fourth nethanel the fifth raddai, the sixth ozem and the seventh david.
Their sisters were zeruiah and abigail. zeruiah and abigil. zeruiahs three sons were abishai, joab, and asahel.
Abigail was the mother of amasa whose father was jether the ishaelite.
Caleb son of hezron

the fatherjair

The sons of noah who came out of the ark were shem, ham, japheth, ham was the father of canaan, these was the three sons of noah, and from them were scattered Over the whole earth.

When noah awoke from his wine and found out what his younger son had done to him he said, curse be canaan the lowest of slaves will he be to his brothers.

He also said, praise be to the lord the god of shem,may canaan be the slave of shem.

May god extend japheth territory,may japheth live in tents of shem and may canaan be the slave of japheth.

Israel by violating the ban on taking devoted things.

The son of ethan;
Azariah
The sons born to hezron were;
Jerahmeel, ram and caleb.
From ram son to hezron
Ram was the father of
Amminadab, and amminadab the father of nahshon, the leader, of the people of judah.
Nahshon was the father of salmon, salmon the father of boaz
Boaz the father of obed and obed the father of jesse .
Jesse was the father of eliab his firstborn ; the second son was abinadab ,the third shimea, the fourth nethanel the fifth raddai, the sixth ozem and the seventh david.
Their sisters were zeruiah and abigail. zeruiah and abigil. zeruiahs three sons were abishai, joab, and asahel.
Abigail was the mother of amasa whose father was jether the ishaelite.
Caleb son of hezron

the fatherjair

After the flood noah lived 350 years noah lived a total of 950 years then he died.

The sons of japheth gomer, magog, madai, javan, tubal, meshek, tiras.

The sons of gomer, ashkenaz, riphath and togarmah.

The sons of javan; elishah, tarshish, the kitties and the rodnites, from these the maritime people spread out into territories by their clans within their nations each with its own language.

The sons of ham cush, egypt, put and canaan

Israel by violating the ban on taking devoted things.

The son of ethan;
Azariah
The sons born to hezron were;
Jerahmeel, ram and caleb.
From ram son to hezron
Ram was the father of
Amminadab, and amminadab the father of nahshon, the leader, of the people of judah.
Nahshon was the father of salmon, salmon the father of boaz
Boaz the father of obed and obed the father of jesse .
Jesse was the father of eliab his firstborn ; the second son was abinadab ,the third shimea, the fourth nethanel the fifth raddai, the sixth ozem and the seventh david.
Their sisters were zeruiah and abigail. zeruiah and abigil. zeruiahs three sons were abishai, joab, and asahel.
Abigail was the mother of amasa whose father was jether the ishaelite.
Caleb son of hezron

the fatherjair

The sons of cush, seba, havilah, sabtah, raamah and sabteka.

The sons of raamah; sheba and dedan.

Cush was the father of nimrod,who became a mighty warrior on earth, he was a mighty hunter before the lord,that is why it is said, like nimrod a mighty hunter before the lord, the first centers of his kingdom was babylon, uruk,akkad, and kalneh,in shinar.

Egypt was the father of the ludites, anamities, lehabites, naphtuhites, pathrusites, kasluhites, from who philistines came,and caphtorites.

Israel by violating the ban on taking devoted things.

The son of ethan;
Azariah
The sons born to hezron were;
Jerahmeel, ram and caleb.
From ram son to hezron
Ram was the father of
Amminadab, and amminadab the father of nahshon, the leader, of the people of judah.
Nahshon was the father of salmon, salmon the father of boaz
Boaz the father of obed and obed the father of jesse .
Jesse was the father of eliab his firstborn ; the second son was abinadab ,the third shimea, the fourth nethanel the fifth raddai, the sixth ozem and the seventh david.
Their sisters were zeruiah and abigail. zeruiah and abigil. zeruiahs three sons were abishai, joab, and asahel.
Abigail was the mother of amasa whose father was jether the ishaelite.
Caleb son of hezron

the fatherjair

Canaan was the father of sidon his firstborn and of the hittites . jebusites, amorites, girgashites, hivites, arkites, sinites, arvadites, zemarites and hamathites.

Later the canaanite clans scattered and the borders of canaan reached from sidon toward gerar as far as gaza, and then toward sodom, gomorrah, admah and, zeboyim as far as lasha, these are the sons of ham, by their clans, and languages,in their territories and nations.

Sons also wae born to shem whose older brothers was japheth; shem was the ancestor of all the sons of eber. The sons of shem, elam, ashur, arphaxad, lud and aram.

The sons of aram; uz,hul,gether and meshek, arphaxad, was the father of shelah and shelah the father of eber; two

Israel by violating the ban on taking devoted things.

The son of ethan;
Azariah
The sons born to hezron were;
Jerahmeel, ram and caleb.
From ram son to hezron
Ram was the father of
Amminadab, and amminadab the father of nahshon, the leader, of the people of judah.
Nahshon was the father of salmon, salmon the father of boaz
Boaz the father of obed and obed the father of jesse .
Jesse was the father of eliab his firstborn ; the second son was abinadab ,the third shimea, the fourth nethanel the fifth raddai, the sixth ozem and the seventh david.
Their sisters were zeruiah and abigail. zeruiah and abigil. zeruiahs three sons were abishai, joab, and asahel.
Abigail was the mother of amasa whose father was jether the ishaelite.
Caleb son of hezron

the fatherjair

sons was born to eber; one was named peleg,because in his time the earth was divided; his brother was named joktan. Joktan was the father of almondad, sheleph, hazarmaveth,jerah, hadoram, uzal, diklah, obal, abimael, sheba,ophir, havilah, and jobab. All these were the sons of joktan.

These are the clans of noah's sons, according to their lines of descent, within their nations, from these the national spread out over the earth after the flood.

The region where they lived stretched from mesba toward sephar, in the eastern hill country.

These are the sons of shem by their clans and languages,in their territories and nations.

Israel by violating the ban on taking devoted things.

The son of ethan;
Azariah
The sons born to hezron were;
Jerahmeel, ram and caleb.
From ram son to hezron
Ram was the father of
Amminadab, and amminadab the father of nahshon, the leader, of the people of judah.
Nahshon was the father of salmon, salmon the father of boaz
Boaz the father of obed and obed the father of jesse .
Jesse was the father of eliab his firstborn ; the second son was abinadab ,the third shimea, the fourth nethanel the fifth raddai, the sixth ozem and the seventh david.
Their sisters were zeruiah and abigail. zeruiah and abigil. zeruiahs three sons were abishai, joab, and asahel.
Abigail was the mother of amasa whose father was jether the ishaelite.
Caleb son of hezron

the fatherjair

The tower of babel

Now the whole world had one language and a common speech, as people moved eastward, they found a plain in shinar,and settled there.they said to each other, come,let us build ourselves a city, with a tower that reaches to heavens, let's make brick and bake them thoroughly they used brick instead of stone. So that we may make a name for ourselves, otherwise we will be scattered over the face of the whole earth. but the lord

Came down to see the city and the tower the people were building, the lord said,if as one people speaking the same language they have begun to do this, then nothing they plan to do will be impossible for them. Let us go down

Israel by violating the ban on taking devoted things.

The son of ethan;
Azariah
The sons born to hezron were;
Jerahmeel, ram and caleb.
From ram son to hezron
Ram was the father of
Amminadab, and amminadab the father of nahshon, the leader, of the people of judah.
Nahshon was the father of salmon, salmon the father of boaz
Boaz the father of obed and obed the father of jesse .
Jesse was the father of eliab his firstborn ; the second son was abinadab ,the third shimea, the fourth nethanel the fifth raddai, the sixth ozem and the seventh david.
Their sisters were zeruiah and abigail. zeruiah and abigil. zeruiahs three sons were abishai, joab, and asahel.
Abigail was the mother of amasa whose father was jether the ishaelite.
Caleb son of hezron

the fatherjair

and confuse their language so they will not understand each other. So the lord scattered them from there over all the earth,and they stop building the city. That is why it was called babel.

When shem was 100 years old two years after the flood,he became the father of arphaxad,and after he became the father of arphaxad, shem lived 500 years and had other sons and daughters. When arphaxad had lived 35 years he became the father of shelah.

And after he became the father of shelah,arphaxad lived 403 years and had other sons and daughters, when shelah lived 30 years he became the father of eber, and after he became the father of eber,shelah lived 403 years and had

---

Israel by violating the ban on taking devoted things.

The son of ethan;
Azariah
The sons born to hezron were;
Jerahmeel, ram and caleb.
From ram son to hezron
Ram was the father of
Amminadab, and amminadab the father of nahshon, the leader, of the people of judah.
Nahshon was the father of salmon, salmon the father of boaz
Boaz the father of obed and obed the father of jesse .
Jesse was the father of eliab his firstborn ; the second son was abinadab ,the third shimea, the fourth nethanel the fifth raddai, the sixth ozem and the seventh david.
Their sisters were zeruiah and abigail. zeruiah and abigil. zeruiahs three sons were abishai, joab, and asahel.
Abigail was the mother of amasa whose father was jether the ishaelite.
Caleb son of hezron

the fatherjair

other sons and daughters . when eber had lived 34 years he became the father of peleg, and after he became the father of peleg, eber lived 430 years and had other sons and daugthers . when peleg had lived 30 years he became the father of reu. After he became the father of reu, peleg lived 209 years and had other sons and daughters . when reu had lived 32 years he became the father of serug,and after he became the father of serug reu lived 207 years and had other sons and daugthers, when serug had lived 30 years he became the father of nahor. Serug lived 200 years and had other sons and daugthers, when nahor had lived 29 years he became the father of terah,and after he became the father of terah, nahor lived 119 years and had other sons and daughters, after terah had lived 70 years he became the father of abram, nahor and haran.

Israel by violating the ban on taking devoted things.

The son of ethan;
Azariah
The sons born to hezron were;
Jerahmeel, ram and caleb.
From ram son to hezron
Ram was the father of
Amminadab, and amminadab the father of nahshon, the leader, of the people of judah.
Nahshon was the father of salmon, salmon the father of boaz
Boaz the father of obed and obed the father of jesse .
Jesse was the father of eliab his firstborn ; the second son was abinadab ,the third shimea, the fourth nethanel the fifth raddai, the sixth ozem and the seventh david.
Their sisters were zeruiah and abigail. zeruiah and abigil. zeruiahs three sons were abishai, joab, and asahel.
Abigail was the mother of amasa whose father was jether the ishaelite.
Caleb son of hezron

the fatherjair

Abram family --------------

This is the account of terah's family line------------------

Terah became the father of abram, nahor and haran . and haran became the father of lot.while his father terah was still alive, haran died in ur of the chaldeans, in the land of his birth, abram and nahor both married the name of abram wife was sarai,and the name of nahor's wife was milkah; she was the daughter of haran,the father of both milkah and iskah . now sarai was childless because she was unable to conceive. Terah took his son abram,his grandson lot, son of haran and his daughter in law sarai,the wife of his son abram,and together they set out for ur, of the chaldeans to go to canaan. But when they came to

---

Israel by violating the ban on taking devoted things.

The son of ethan;
Azariah
The sons born to hezron were;
Jerahmeel, ram and caleb.
From ram son to hezron
Ram was the father of
Amminadab, and amminadab the father of nahshon, the leader, of the people of judah.
Nahshon was the father of salmon, salmon the father of boaz
Boaz the father of obed and obed the father of jesse .
Jesse was the father of eliab his firstborn ; the second son was abinadab ,the third shimea, the fourth nethanel the fifth raddai, the sixth ozem and the seventh david.
Their sisters were zeruiah and abigail. zeruiah and abigil. zeruiahs three sons were abishai, joab, and asahel.
Abigail was the mother of amasa whose father was jether the ishaelite.
Caleb son of hezron

the fatherjair

harran,they settled there. Terah lived 205 years and he died in harran.

The call of abram----------------

Abram was seventy-five years old when he set out from harran,he took his wife sarai and his nephew lot, when abram came to egypt, the egyptians saw that sarai was a very beautiful woman, and when pharaoh's officials,they praised her to pharaoh . and she was taken into his palace. He treated abram well for her sake, abram warned saria to say she was his sister otherwise pharaoh will kill him .abram acquired sheep and cattle,male and female donkeys, male and female servants and camels. But the lord inflicted serious diseases on pharaoh and his household because

Israel by violating the ban on taking devoted things.

The son of ethan;
Azariah
The sons born to hezron were;
Jerahmeel, ram and caleb.
From ram son to hezron
Ram was the father of
Amminadab, and amminadab the father of nahshon, the leader, of the people of judah.
Nahshon was the father of salmon, salmon the father of boaz
Boaz the father of obed and obed the father of jesse .
Jesse was the father of eliab his firstborn ; the second son was abinadab ,the third shimea, the fourth nethanel the fifth raddai, the sixth ozem and the seventh david.
Their sisters were zeruiah and abigail. zeruiah and abigil. zeruiahs three sons were abishai, joab, and asahel.
Abigail was the mother of amasa whose father was jether the ishaelite.
Caleb son of hezron

the fatherjair

of abram wife sarai.so pharaoh summoned abram. What have you done to me he said,why didn't you tell me she was your wife,why did you say she is my sister, that i took her to be my wife,now then here is your wife take her and go. So abram went up from egypt to the negev with his wife and everything he had,and lot went with him, abram had become very wealthy in livestock and in silver and gold.

From the negev he went from place to place until he came to bethel, the place between bethel and ai where his tent had been earlier, and where he had first built an altar, there abram called on the name of the lord. Lot looked around and saw the whole plain of jordan toward zoar was well watered, like the garden of the lord,like the

---

Israel by violating the ban on taking devoted things.

The son of ethan;
Azariah
The sons born to hezron were;
Jerahmeel, ram and caleb.
From ram son to hezron
Ram was the father of
Amminadab, and amminadab the father of nahshon, the leader, of the people of judah.
Nahshon was the father of salmon, salmon the father of boaz
Boaz the father of obed and obed the father of jesse .
Jesse was the father of eliab his firstborn ; the second son was abinadab ,the third shimea, the fourth nethanel the fifth raddai, the sixth ozem and the seventh david.
Their sisters were zeruiah and abigail. zeruiah and abigil. zeruiahs three sons were abishai, joab, and asahel.
Abigail was the mother of amasa whose father was jether the ishaelite.
Caleb son of hezron

the fatherjair

land of egypt .this was before the lord destroyed sodom and gomorrah, so lot chose for himself the whole plain of jordan and set out toward the east . the two men parted company abram lived in the land of canaan,while lot lived among the cities of the plain and pitched his tents near sodom. Now the people of sodom were wicked and were sinning greatly against the lord. So abram went to live near the great trees of mamre at hebron where he pitched his tents there he built an altar to the lord. The four kings seized all the goods of sodom and gomorrah and all their food then they went away,they also carried off abraham's nephew lot and his possessions .since he was living in sodom,

Israel by violating the ban on taking devoted things.

The son of ethan;
Azariah
The sons born to hezron were;
Jerahmeel, ram and caleb.
From ram son to hezron
Ram was the father of
Amminadab, and amminadab the father of nahshon, the leader, of the people of judah.
Nahshon was the father of salmon, salmon the father of boaz
Boaz the father of obed and obed the father of jesse .
Jesse was the father of eliab his firstborn ; the second son was abinadab ,the third shimea, the fourth nethanel the fifth raddai, the sixth ozem and the seventh david.
Their sisters were zeruiah and abigail. zeruiah and abigil. zeruiahs three sons were abishai, joab, and asahel.
Abigail was the mother of amasa whose father was jether the ishaelite.
Caleb son of hezron

the fatherjair

A man who had escaped came and reported this to abram the hebrew. Now abram was living near the great trees of mamre the amorite a brother of eshcol and aner, all of whom were allied with abram . when abram heard that his relative had been taken captive, he called out 318 trained men born in his household and went in pursuit as far as dan.

During the night abram divided his men to attack them and he routed them, pursuing them as far as hobah, north of damascus . he recovered all the goods and brought back relative lot and his possessions, together with the woman and other people .after abram returned from defeating kedorlaomer and the kings allied with him, the king of sodom came came out to meet him in the valley of

---

Israel by violating the ban on taking devoted things.

The son of ethan;
Azariah
The sons born to hezron were;
Jerahmeel, ram and caleb.
From ram son to hezron
Ram was the father of
Amminadab, and amminadab the father of nahshon, the leader, of the people of judah.
Nahshon was the father of salmon, salmon the father of boaz
Boaz the father of obed and obed the father of jesse .
Jesse was the father of eliab his firstborn ; the second son was abinadab ,the third shimea, the fourth nethanel the fifth raddai, the sixth ozem and the seventh david.
Their sisters were zeruiah and abigail. zeruiah and abigil. zeruiahs three sons were abishai, joab, and asahel.
Abigail was the mother of amasa whose father was jether the ishaelite.
Caleb son of hezron

the fatherjair

shaveh -- that is the kings valley, then melchizedek king of salem brought out bread and wine . he was priest of god the most high and he blessed abram, saying, bless be abraham by god the most high, who delivered your enemies into your hand. After this,the word of the lord came to abram in a vision; do not be afraid,abram i am your shield, your very great reward. But abram said,'sovereign lord, what can you give me since i remain childless and the one who will inherit my estate is eliezer of damascus?

As the sun was setting abram fell into a deep sleep, and a thick and dreadful darkness came over him . then the lord said to him, known for certain that for four hundred years your descendants will be strangers in a country not their own and that they will be enslaved and mistreated there,

---

Israel by violating the ban on taking devoted things.

The son of ethan;
Azariah
The sons born to hezron were;
Jerahmeel, ram and caleb.
From ram son to hezron
Ram was the father of
Amminadab, and amminadab the father of nahshon, the leader, of the people of judah.
Nahshon was the father of salmon, salmon the father of boaz
Boaz the father of obed and obed the father of jesse .
Jesse was the father of eliab his firstborn ; the second son was abinadab ,the third shimea, the fourth nethanel the fifth raddai, the sixth ozem and the seventh david.
Their sisters were zeruiah and abigail. zeruiah and abigil. zeruiahs three sons were abishai, joab, and asahel.
Abigail was the mother of amasa whose father was jether the ishaelite.
Caleb son of hezron

the fatherjair

but i will punish the nation that they serve as slaves and afterward they will come out with great possessions . you however will go to your ancestors in peace and be buried at a good old age in the fourth generation

Your descendants will come back here, for the sin of the amorites they has not yet reached its full measures. When the sun had set and darkness had fallen a smoking firepot with a blazing torch appeared and passed between the pieces,on that day the lord a covenant with abram and said,to your descendants,i will give this land from the wadi of egypt to the great river, the euphrates ------the land of kenites, kenizzites, kadmonites, hittites, perizzites, rephaites, amorites, canaanites, girgashites, and jebsites.

Israel by violating the ban on taking devoted things.

The son of ethan;
Azariah
The sons born to hezron were;
Jerahmeel, ram and caleb.
From ram son to hezron
Ram was the father of
Amminadab, and amminadab the father of nahshon, the leader, of the people of judah.
Nahshon was the father of salmon, salmon the father of boaz
Boaz the father of obed and obed the father of jesse .
Jesse was the father of eliab his firstborn ; the second son was abinadab ,the third shimea, the fourth nethanel the fifth raddai, the sixth ozem and the seventh david.
Their sisters were zeruiah and abigail. zeruiah and abigil. zeruiahs three sons were abishai, joab, and asahel.
Abigail was the mother of amasa whose father was jether the ishaelite.
Caleb son of hezron

the fatherjair

Now sarai abram wife,had borne him no children. but she had an egyptian slave name hagar, so she said to abram, the lord has kept me having children. go sleep with my slave ' perhaps i can build a family through her. Abram agreed to what sarai said, after abram slept with hagar and she conceived. She gave birth to a son named ishmael.

When abram was ninety -nine years old the lord appeared to him and said i am god almighty, walk before me and be faithfully and be blameless, then i will make my covenant between me and you and will greatly lncrease your numbers. Abram felled face down, and god said to him,as for as for me this is my covenant with you. You will be the father of many nations, no longer will you be called abram,your name will be abraham, for i have made you the

Israel by violating the ban on taking devoted things.

The son of ethan;
Azariah
The sons born to hezron were;
Jerahmeel, ram and caleb.
From ram son to hezron
Ram was the father of
Amminadab, and amminadab the father of nahshon, the leader, of the people of judah.
Nahshon was the father of salmon, salmon the father of boaz
Boaz the father of obed and obed the father of jesse .
Jesse was the father of eliab his firstborn ; the second son was abinadab ,the third shimea, the fourth nethanel the fifth raddai, the sixth ozem and the seventh david.
Their sisters were zeruiah and abigail. zeruiah and abigil. zeruiahs three sons were abishai, joab, and asahel.
Abigail was the mother of amasa whose father was jether the ishaelite.
Caleb son of hezron

the fatherjair

father of many nations, i will make you very fruitful i will make nations of you and kings will come from you, i will establish my covenant as a everlasting covenant between you and me and your descendants for the generations to come,to be your god and the god of your descendants after you. The whole land of canaan where you will reside as a foreigner.i will give as a everlasting possession to you and your descendants after you for the generations to come.to be your god and the god of your descendants. every male among you shall be circumcised. Every male among you who is eight days old must be circumcised. Including those born in your household or brought with money from a foreigner.

Israel by violating the ban on taking devoted things.

The son of ethan;
Azariah
The sons born to hezron were;
Jerahmeel, ram and caleb.
From ram son to hezron
Ram was the father of
Amminadab, and amminadab the father of nahshon, the leader, of the people of judah.
Nahshon was the father of salmon, salmon the father of boaz
Boaz the father of obed and obed the father of jesse .
Jesse was the father of eliab his firstborn ; the second son was abinadab ,the third shimea, the fourth nethanel the fifth raddai, the sixth ozem and the seventh david.
Their sisters were zeruiah and abigail. zeruiah and abigil. zeruiahs three sons were abishai, joab, and asahel.
Abigail was the mother of amasa whose father was jether the ishaelite.
Caleb son of hezron

the fatherjair

Those who is not your offspring. as for sarai your wife,you are no longer to call her sarai her name will be sarah, i will bless her and surely give you a son by her. I will bless her so that she will be the mother of nations. kings of people will come from her abraham fell to his face down he laughed and said himself will a son be born to a man one hundred years old, will sarah give birth to a son ninety years old,if only ishmael would live under your blessings.then god said yes but your wife sarah will bear you a son. And you will call him isaac, and as for ishmael i have heard you i will make him fruitful and will greatly increase his numbers he will be the father of twelve rulers.

Circumcised-------- opening my eyes to see my government who is closed on sunday and the sabbath ------i

Israel by violating the ban on taking devoted things.

The son of ethan;
Azariah
The sons born to hezron were;
Jerahmeel, ram and caleb.
From ram son to hezron
Ram was the father of
Amminadab, and amminadab the father of nahshon, the leader, of the people of judah.
Nahshon was the father of salmon, salmon the father of boaz
Boaz the father of obed and obed the father of jesse .
Jesse was the father of eliab his firstborn ; the second son was abinadab ,the third shimea, the fourth nethanel the fifth raddai, the sixth ozem and the seventh david.
Their sisters were zeruiah and abigail. zeruiah and abigil. zeruiahs three sons were abishai, joab, and asahel.
Abigail was the mother of amasa whose father was jether the ishaelite.
Caleb son of hezron

the fatherjair

notice threw and oath in the united state's court's they use a bible also circumcised is here and throughout america down to my son even further. abraham generation is very big.

Abraham had taken another wife whose name was keturah, she bore him zimran, jokshan, medan, midian, ishbak, and shuah. Jokshan was the father of sheba and dedan the descendant of dedan were the ashurites. The letushites and the leummites. The sons of midian were ephah, epher, hanok, abida and eldaah, all these were descendants of keturah.

Ishmael son's-------------

Israel by violating the ban on taking devoted things.

The son of ethan;
Azariah
The sons born to hezron were;
Jerahmeel, ram and caleb.
From ram son to hezron
Ram was the father of
Amminadab, and amminadab the father of nahshon, the leader, of the people of judah.
Nahshon was the father of salmon, salmon the father of boaz
Boaz the father of obed and obed the father of jesse .
Jesse was the father of eliab his firstborn ; the second son was abinadab ,the third shimea, the fourth nethanel the fifth raddai, the sixth ozem and the seventh david.
Their sisters were zeruiah and abigail. zeruiah and abigil. zeruiahs three sons were abishai, joab, and asahel.
Abigail was the mother of amasa whose father was jether the ishaelite.
Caleb son of hezron

the fatherjair

Hagar the egyptian bore to abraham ishmael who bore sons

Nebaioth, kedar, adbeel, mibsam, mishma, dumah, massa, hadad,tema, jetur, naphish,and kedemah. These were the sons of ishmael,and these were the names of twelve tribes

Rulers according to their settlements and camps.ishmael lived one hundred and thirty seven he breathed his last and died.

Isaac was forty years when he married rebekah the daughter of bethuel the aramean from paddan aram and sister of laban the aramean.

Israel by violating the ban on taking devoted things.

The son of ethan;
Azariah
The sons born to hezron were;
Jerahmeel, ram and caleb.
From ram son to hezron
Ram was the father of
Amminadab, and amminadab the father of nahshon, the leader, of the people of judah.
Nahshon was the father of salmon, salmon the father of boaz
Boaz the father of obed and obed the father of jesse .
Jesse was the father of eliab his firstborn ; the second son was abinadab ,the third shimea, the fourth nethanel the fifth raddai, the sixth ozem and the seventh david.
Their sisters were zeruiah and abigail. zeruiah and abigil. zeruiahs three sons were abishai, joab, and asahel.
Abigail was the mother of amasa whose father was jether the ishaelite.
Caleb son of hezron

the fatherjair

Two nations were in the womb of rebekah, two twin boys the first one came out red and like a hairy garment. After this his brother came out with his hand grasping esau's heel so he was named jacob. Esau and jacob.

Genesis 26 -5 because abraham obeyed me and did everything i required of him keeping my commands, my decrees and my instructions.

Jacob married leah and rachel now laban had two daughters, the name of the oldest was leah and the name of the younger was rachel

Leah named her son reuben. She birth another son she named him simeon, again she conceived levi. and judah

---

Israel by violating the ban on taking devoted things.

The son of ethan;
Azariah
The sons born to hezron were;
Jerahmeel, ram and caleb.
From ram son to hezron
Ram was the father of
Amminadab, and amminadab the father of nahshon, the leader, of the people of judah.
Nahshon was the father of salmon, salmon the father of boaz
Boaz the father of obed and obed the father of jesse .
Jesse was the father of eliab his firstborn ; the second son was abinadab ,the third shimea, the fourth nethanel the fifth raddai, the sixth ozem and the seventh david.
Their sisters were zeruiah and abigail. zeruiah and abigil. zeruiahs three sons were abishai, joab, and asahel.
Abigail was the mother of amasa whose father was jether the ishaelite.
Caleb son of hezron

the fatherjair

Bilhah was a servant wife given to jacob

By rachel to bear her a family she could not bear she named the son dan, leah took her servant zilpah to bear her a son she named him gad. Then asher was born, issachar was born by leah,

Zebulun was born,she gave birth to a daughter named dinah .rachel god enabled to conceive a son she named joseph . rachel said to her father don't be angry my lord that i cannot stand up in your presence; i'm having my period. Jacob name was changed to israel.

Therefore to this day the israelites do not eat the tendon attached to the socket of the hip because the socket of jacob's hip was touched near the tendon.

Israel by violating the ban on taking devoted things.

The son of ethan;
Azariah
The sons born to hezron were;
Jerahmeel, ram and caleb.
From ram son to hezron
Ram was the father of
Amminadab, and amminadab the father of nahshon, the leader, of the people of judah.
Nahshon was the father of salmon, salmon the father of boaz
Boaz the father of obed and obed the father of jesse .
Jesse was the father of eliab his firstborn ; the second son was abinadab ,the third shimea, the fourth nethanel the fifth raddai, the sixth ozem and the seventh david.
Their sisters were zeruiah and abigail. zeruiah and abigil. zeruiahs three sons were abishai, joab, and asahel.
Abigail was the mother of amasa whose father was jether the ishaelite.
Caleb son of hezron

the fatherjair

Rachel began to give birth and had great difficulty she had another son ben-oni, but his father named him benjamin,so rachel died and was buried on the way to ephrath, that is bethlehem.jacob had twelve son's, the sons of leah, reuben the firstborn, simeon, levi,judah,issachar, and zebulun. The sons of rachel, joseph and benjamin, the sons of rachel's servant bilhad; dan,and naphtali, the sons of leah's servant zilpah,gad and asher.

Isaac lived a hundred and eighty years then he died.

These are the names of esau's sons --------eliphaz,the son of esau's wife adah and reuel,the sons of esau's wife basemath, the sons of eliphar; teman, omar, zepho, gatam and kenaz.

Israel by violating the ban on taking devoted things.

The son of ethan;
Azariah
The sons born to hezron were;
Jerahmeel, ram and caleb.
From ram son to hezron
Ram was the father of
Amminadab, and amminadab the father of nahshon, the leader, of the people of judah.
Nahshon was the father of salmon, salmon the father of boaz
Boaz the father of obed and obed the father of jesse .
Jesse was the father of eliab his firstborn ; the second son was abinadab ,the third shimea, the fourth nethanel the fifth raddai, the sixth ozem and the seventh david.
Their sisters were zeruiah and abigail. zeruiah and abigil. zeruiahs three sons were abishai, joab, and asahel.
Abigail was the mother of amasa whose father was jether the ishaelite.
Caleb son of hezron

the fatherjair

Timna who bore elipaz, amalek these were the grandson s of esau's wife adah.

The son's of reuel, naahath zerah shammah and mizzah these were grandsons of esau's wife basemath .the son's of esau's wife oholibamah daughter of anah and granddaughter of zibeon,whom she bore to esau,jeush, jalam and korah.chief's teman, chiefs nahath zerah, shammah and mizzah, chiehs descended from esau's wife oholibamah daughter of anah. These were the son's of esau's that is edom and these were their chiefs. These were the sons of seir the horite, who were living in the region; lotan shobal, zibeon anah, dishon,ezer and dishan these sons of seir in edom were horite chiefs.the son's of lotan Hori and homam. Timna was lotan's sister. The

Israel by violating the ban on taking devoted things.

The son of ethan;
Azariah
The sons born to hezron were;
Jerahmeel, ram and caleb.
From ram son to hezron
Ram was the father of
Amminadab, and amminadab the father of nahshon, the leader, of the people of judah.
Nahshon was the father of salmon, salmon the father of boaz
Boaz the father of obed and obed the father of jesse .
Jesse was the father of eliab his firstborn ; the second son was abinadab ,the third shimea, the fourth nethanel the fifth raddai, the sixth ozem and the seventh david.
Their sisters were zeruiah and abigail. zeruiah and abigil. zeruiahs three sons were abishai, joab, and asahel.
Abigail was the mother of amasa whose father was jether the ishaelite.
Caleb son of hezron

the fatherjair

son's of shobal; alvan, manahath, ebal, shepho and onam. The son's of zibeon alah and anah, this is the anah who discovered the hot springs in the desert while he was grazing the donkey of his father zibeon. The children of anah; dishon and oholibamah daughter of anah, the son's of dishon hemdan, eshban, ithran, and keran . the son's of ezer; bilan, zaavan and akan. Uz, and aran, these were the horite chiefs

Lotan, shobal, zibeon,anah, dishon, ezer and dishan, these were the horite chiefs according to their divisions, in the land of seir.

These were the kings who reigned in edom before any israelite king reigned;

Israel by violating the ban on taking devoted things.

The son of ethan;
Azariah
The sons born to hezron were;
Jerahmeel, ram and caleb.
From ram son to hezron
Ram was the father of
Amminadab, and amminadab the father of nahshon, the leader, of the people of judah.
Nahshon was the father of salmon, salmon the father of boaz
Boaz the father of obed and obed the father of jesse .
Jesse was the father of eliab his firstborn ; the second son was abinadab ,the third shimea, the fourth nethanel the fifth raddai, the sixth ozem and the seventh david.
Their sisters were zeruiah and abigail. zeruiah and abigil. zeruiahs three sons were abishai, joab, and asahel.
Abigail was the mother of amasa whose father was jether the ishaelite.
Caleb son of hezron

the fatherjair

Bela son of beor became king of edom . his city was named dinhabah.

When bela died jobab son of zerah from bozrah succeeded him as king . when jobab died, husham from the land land of temanites succeeded him as king.

When husham died hadad son of bedad who defeated midian in the country of moah, succeeded him as king,his city was named avith. When hadad died samiah from masrekah succeeded him as king . when samiah died, shaul from rehoboth on the river succeeded him as king. When shaul died baal-hanan son of akbor succeeded him as king when baal-hanan died hadad succeeded him as

Israel by violating the ban on taking devoted things.

The son of ethan;
Azariah
The sons born to hezron were;
Jerahmeel, ram and caleb.
From ram son to hezron
Ram was the father of
Amminadab, and amminadab the father of nahshon, the leader, of the people of judah.
Nahshon was the father of salmon, salmon the father of boaz
Boaz the father of obed and obed the father of jesse .
Jesse was the father of eliab his firstborn ; the second son was abinadab ,the third shimea, the fourth nethanel the fifth raddai, the sixth ozem and the seventh david.
Their sisters were zeruiah and abigail. zeruiah and abigil. zeruiahs three sons were abishai, joab, and asahel.
Abigail was the mother of amasa whose father was jether the ishaelite.
Caleb son of hezron

the fatherjair

king his city was named pau and his wife name was mehetabel daughter of matred the daughter of me-zahab.

These were the chiefs descended from esau,by name according to their clans and regions.

Timna, alvan, jetheth. Oholibamah, elah,pinon, kenaz, teman, mibzar, magdiel, and iram.

These were the chiefs of edom, according to their settlements in the land they occupied.

This is the family line of esau, the father of edomites.

Jacob lived in the land where his father had stayed, the land of canaan.

Israel by violating the ban on taking devoted things.

The son of ethan;
Azariah
The sons born to hezron were;
Jerahmeel, ram and caleb.
From ram son to hezron
Ram was the father of
Amminadab, and amminadab the father of nahshon, the leader, of the people of judah.
Nahshon was the father of salmon, salmon the father of boaz
Boaz the father of obed and obed the father of jesse .
Jesse was the father of eliab his firstborn ; the second son was abinadab ,the third shimea, the fourth nethanel the fifth raddai, the sixth ozem and the seventh david.
Their sisters were zeruiah and abigail. zeruiah and abigil. zeruiahs three sons were abishai, joab, and asahel.
Abigail was the mother of amasa whose father was jether the ishaelite.
Caleb son of hezron

the fatherjair

This is account of jacob family.

Joseph, a young man of seventeen was tending the flock with his brothers the son of bilhah and the sons of zilpah, his father's wives, and he brought their father a bad report about them.

Pharaoh made joseph in charge of the whole land of egypt, he named joseph zaphenath -paneah, pharaoh gave him asenath daughter of potiphera, two son's was born to joseph,manasseh and ephraim.

Now a man of the tribe levi, married a levi woman and she became pregnant and gave birth to a son, when she saw that he was a fine child, she hid him for three months,

---

Israel by violating the ban on taking devoted things.

The son of ethan;
Azariah
The sons born to hezron were;
Jerahmeel, ram and caleb.
From ram son to hezron
Ram was the father of
Amminadab, and amminadab the father of nahshon, the leader, of the people of judah.
Nahshon was the father of salmon, salmon the father of boaz
Boaz the father of obed and obed the father of jesse .
Jesse was the father of eliab his firstborn ; the second son was abinadab ,the third shimea, the fourth nethanel the fifth raddai, the sixth ozem and the seventh david.
Their sisters were zeruiah and abigail. zeruiah and abigil. zeruiahs three sons were abishai, joab, and asahel.
Abigail was the mother of amasa whose father was jether the ishaelite.
Caleb son of hezron

the fatherjair

but when she could hide him no longer, she got a papyrus basket for him and coated it with tar and pitch.

Then she placed the child in it and put it among the reeds alone the bank of nile.

His sister stood at a distance to see what would happened to him, then pharaoh's daughter went down to nile to bathe, and her attendants were walking along the river bank.

She saw the basket among the reeds and sent her female slaves to get it, she opened it and saw the baby, he was crying and she felt sorry for him, this is one of the hebrew babies she said,then his sister asked pharaoh's daughter, shall i go and get one of the hebrew woman to nurse the

---

Israel by violating the ban on taking devoted things.

The son of ethan;
Azariah
The sons born to hezron were;
Jerahmeel, ram and caleb.
From ram son to hezron
Ram was the father of
Amminadab, and amminadab the father of nahshon, the leader, of the people of judah.
Nahshon was the father of salmon, salmon the father of boaz
Boaz the father of obed and obed the father of jesse .
Jesse was the father of eliab his firstborn ; the second son was abinadab ,the third shimea, the fourth nethanel the fifth raddai, the sixth ozem and the seventh david.
Their sisters were zeruiah and abigail. zeruiah and abigil. zeruiahs three sons were abishai, joab, and asahel.
Abigail was the mother of amasa whose father was jether the ishaelite.
Caleb son of hezron

the fatherjair

baby for you, yes go, she answered, so the girl went and got the baby's mother. Pharaods daughter said to her take this baby and nurse him for me, and i will pay you, so the took the baby and nursed him. When the child grew older she took him to pharaod's daughter and he became her son, she named him moses, saying i drew him out of water.

Moses agree to stay with a man, who gave his daughter zipporah to moses in marriage, zipporah gave birth to a son, moses named him gershom saying i become foreigner in a foreign land.

During this period the king of egypt died . the israelites groaned in their slavery and cried out. And their cry

Israel by violating the ban on taking devoted things.

The son of ethan;
Azariah
The sons born to hezron were;
Jerahmeel, ram and caleb.
From ram son to hezron
Ram was the father of
Amminadab, and amminadab the father of nahshon, the leader, of the people of judah.
Nahshon was the father of salmon, salmon the father of boaz
Boaz the father of obed and obed the father of jesse .
Jesse was the father of eliab his firstborn ; the second son was abinadab ,the third shimea, the fourth nethanel the fifth raddai, the sixth ozem and the seventh david.
Their sisters were zeruiah and abigail. zeruiah and abigil. zeruiahs three sons were abishai, joab, and asahel.
Abigail was the mother of amasa whose father was jether the ishaelite.
Caleb son of hezron

the fatherjair

for help because of their slavery went up to god. God heard their groaning and he remembered his covenant with abraham, with issac and jacob so god looked on the israelites and was concerned about them.

Now moses was tending the flock of jethro his father-in-law, the priest of midian, and he led the flock to the far side of the wilderness and came to horeb, the mountain of god. there the angels of the lord appeared to him in flames of fire from within a bush, moses saw that though The bush was on fire it did not burn up . so moses thought, i will go over and see this strange sight -----why the bush does not burn up. When the lord saw that he had went over to look, god called him from within the bush, moses ! moses! And moses said, here i am, do not come any closer, god

Israel by violating the ban on taking devoted things.

The son of ethan;
Azariah
The sons born to hezron were;
Jerahmeel, ram and caleb.
From ram son to hezron
Ram was the father of
Amminadab, and amminadab the father of nahshon, the leader, of the people of judah.
Nahshon was the father of salmon, salmon the father of boaz
Boaz the father of obed and obed the father of jesse .
Jesse was the father of eliab his firstborn ; the second son was abinadab ,the third shimea, the fourth nethanel the fifth raddai, the sixth ozem and the seventh david.
Their sisters were zeruiah and abigail. zeruiah and abigil. zeruiahs three sons were abishai, joab, and asahel.
Abigail was the mother of amasa whose father was jether the ishaelite.
Caleb son of hezron

the fatherjair

said,god said take take off your sandals,for the place you are standing is holy ground . then he said, i am the god of your father. The god of abraham,the god of isaac,and the god of jacob .at this moses hid his face,because he was afraid to look at god. God said to moses iam who iam this is what you is to say to the israelites. The lord the god of your father-------the god of abraham the god of issac and the god of jacob ----has sent me to you . this is my name forever, the name you shall call me from generation to generation.

Moses answered,what if they don't believe me or listen to me and say. The lord did not appear to you? Then the lord said to him, what is that in your hand? A staff he replied.

Israel by violating the ban on taking devoted things.

The son of ethan;
Azariah
The sons born to hezron were;
Jerahmeel, ram and caleb.
From ram son to hezron
Ram was the father of
Amminadab, and amminadab the father of nahshon, the leader, of the people of judah.
Nahshon was the father of salmon, salmon the father of boaz
Boaz the father of obed and obed the father of jesse .
Jesse was the father of eliab his firstborn ; the second son was abinadab ,the third shimea, the fourth nethanel the fifth raddai, the sixth ozem and the seventh david.
Their sisters were zeruiah and abigail. zeruiah and abigil. zeruiahs three sons were abishai, joab, and asahel.
Abigail was the mother of amasa whose father was jether the ishaelite.
Caleb son of hezron

the fatherjair

The lord said throw it there on the ground and it became a snake and he ran from it,the lord said to him reach out your hand and take it by the tail, so moses reached out and took hold of the snake and it turned back into a staff in his hand. This, said the lord is so that they may believe that the lord, the god of their fathers-----the god of abraham, the god of isaac and the god of jacob has appeared to you. Then the lord said put your hand into your cloak. So moses put his hand into his cloak, and when he took it out,the skin was leprous----it had become as white as snow. Now put your hand back into the cloak,moses put his hand back into the cloak, and when he took it out it was restored like the rest of his flesh. If they do not believe you or pay attention to the first sign they may believe the second . but if they do not believe these two signs or

Israel by violating the ban on taking devoted things.

The son of ethan;
Azariah
The sons born to hezron were;
Jerahmeel, ram and caleb.
From ram son to hezron
Ram was the father of
Amminadab, and amminadab the father of nahshon, the leader, of the people of judah.
Nahshon was the father of salmon, salmon the father of boaz
Boaz the father of obed and obed the father of jesse .
Jesse was the father of eliab his firstborn ; the second son was abinadab ,the third shimea, the fourth nethanel the fifth raddai, the sixth ozem and the seventh david.
Their sisters were zeruiah and abigail. zeruiah and abigil. zeruiahs three sons were abishai, joab, and asahel.
Abigail was the mother of amasa whose father was jether the ishaelite.
Caleb son of hezron

the fatherjair

listen to you, take some water from the nile and pour it on the dry ground . the water you take from the river will become blood on the ground .now go said the lord i will help you speak, and teach you what to say. His brother aaron the levite is already on his way to meet moses.the sons of reuben the firstborn son of israel were hanok and pallu, herzron son of israel were hanok and pallu, hezron and karmi. These were the clan of reuben .the sons of simeon were jemuel, jamin, ohad, jakin, zohar, and shaul the sons of a canaanite woman,these were the clans of simeon .these were the names and sons of levi,according to their records gershon,kohath, and merari. Levi lived 137 years the sons of gershon,by clans were libni and shimei. The sons of kohath were amram,izhar,hebron and uzziel, kohath lived 133 years . the sons of merari were

---

Israel by violating the ban on taking devoted things.

The son of ethan;
Azariah
The sons born to hezron were;
Jerahmeel, ram and caleb.
From ram son to hezron
Ram was the father of
Amminadab, and amminadab the father of nahshon, the leader, of the people of judah.
Nahshon was the father of salmon, salmon the father of boaz
Boaz the father of obed and obed the father of jesse .
Jesse was the father of eliab his firstborn ; the second son was abinadab ,the third shimea, the fourth nethanel the fifth raddai, the sixth ozem and the seventh david.
Their sisters were zeruiah and abigail. zeruiah and abigil. zeruiahs three sons were abishai, joab, and asahel.
Abigail was the mother of amasa whose father was jether the ishaelite.
Caleb son of hezron

the fatherjair

mahli and mushi.these were the clans of levi according to their records. Amram married his father's sister jochebed, who bore him aaron and moses .amram lived 137 years . the son of izhar were korah,nepheg, and zikri,the sons of uzziel were mishael, elzaphan and sithri . aaron married elisheba,daughter of putiel and she bore him phinehas.

These were the heads of the levite families,clan by clan.

It was this aaron and moses to whom the lord said. Bring the israelites out of egypt by their divisions'.they were the ones who spoke to pharaoh king of egypt about bringing the israelites out of egypt--this same moses and aaron. Then the lord said to moses,see i have made you like a god to pharaoh and your brother aaron will be your

---

Israel by violating the ban on taking devoted things.

The son of ethan;
Azariah
The sons born to hezron were;
Jerahmeel, ram and caleb.
From ram son to hezron
Ram was the father of
Amminadab, and amminadab the father of nahshon, the leader, of the people of judah.
Nahshon was the father of salmon, salmon the father of boaz
Boaz the father of obed and obed the father of jesse .
Jesse was the father of eliab his firstborn ; the second son was abinadab ,the third shimea, the fourth nethanel the fifth raddai, the sixth ozem and the seventh david.
Their sisters were zeruiah and abigail. zeruiah and abigil. zeruiahs three sons were abishai, joab, and asahel.
Abigail was the mother of amasa whose father was jether the ishaelite.
Caleb son of hezron

the fatherjair

prophet. Aaron's staff became a snake, yet pharaoh's heart became hard and he would not listen to them, just as the lord had said,

The plague of blood, with the staff that is in my hand i will strike the water of nile,and it will be changed into blood,the fish in the nile will die,and the river will stink. The fish in the nile will die the egyptians will not be able to drink it's water. The lord said to moses 'tell aaron,take your staff and stretch over the waters of egypt over the streams and canals,over the ponds and all the reservoirs ------and they will turn to blood,blood will be everywhere,even in vessels' of wood and stone.

Israel by violating the ban on taking devoted things.

The son of ethan;
Azariah
The sons born to hezron were;
Jerahmeel, ram and caleb.
From ram son to hezron
Ram was the father of
Amminadab, and amminadab the father of nahshon, the leader, of the people of judah.
Nahshon was the father of salmon, salmon the father of boaz
Boaz the father of obed and obed the father of jesse .
Jesse was the father of eliab his firstborn ; the second son was abinadab ,the third shimea, the fourth nethanel the fifth raddai, the sixth ozem and the seventh david.
Their sisters were zeruiah and abigail. zeruiah and abigil. zeruiahs three sons were abishai, joab, and asahel.
Abigail was the mother of amasa whose father was jether the ishaelite.
Caleb son of hezron

the fatherjair

In the u.s.a of america also 1989 alaska oil spill fish were dead everywhere also in the five great lakes.

Plague seemed to come every were the plague of frogs covered hawaii
Plagues of flies in east orange new jersey, 1999.
Plague of gnats
Plague of boils
Plague of hail
Plague of locusts
Plague of darkness
Plague on the firstborn

During the night pharaoh summoned moses and aaron and said,up! Leave my people you and the israelites ! go

---

Israel by violating the ban on taking devoted things.

The son of ethan;
Azariah
The sons born to hezron were;
Jerahmeel, ram and caleb.
From ram son to hezron
Ram was the father of
Amminadab, and amminadab the father of nahshon, the leader, of the people of judah.
Nahshon was the father of salmon, salmon the father of boaz
Boaz the father of obed and obed the father of jesse .
Jesse was the father of eliab his firstborn ; the second son was abinadab ,the third shimea, the fourth nethanel the fifth raddai, the sixth ozem and the seventh david.
Their sisters were zeruiah and abigail. zeruiah and abigil. zeruiahs three sons were abishai, joab, and asahel.
Abigail was the mother of amasa whose father was jether the ishaelite.
Caleb son of hezron

the fatherjair

worship the lord you requested. Take your flocks and herbs,as have said and go and also bless me.

There were about six hundred thousand men on feet besides women and children .and many other people went up with them. Israelites People lived 430 years length in egypt

Israelites are to keep vigil to honor the lord for the generations to come.

Moses took the bones of joseph with him,because joseph has made the israelites swear an oath he has said surely your god will come and take you up from this place when he do take my bones with you.

Israel by violating the ban on taking devoted things.

The son of ethan;
Azariah
The sons born to hezron were;
Jerahmeel, ram and caleb.
From ram son to hezron
Ram was the father of
Amminadab, and amminadab the father of nahshon, the leader, of the people of judah.
Nahshon was the father of salmon, salmon the father of boaz
Boaz the father of obed and obed the father of jesse .
Jesse was the father of eliab his firstborn ; the second son was abinadab ,the third shimea, the fourth nethanel the fifth raddai, the sixth ozem and the seventh david.
Their sisters were zeruiah and abigail. zeruiah and abigil. zeruiahs three sons were abishai, joab, and asahel.
Abigail was the mother of amasa whose father was jether the ishaelite.
Caleb son of hezron

the fatherjair

The lord will fight for you, you only need to be still.

Then the lord said to moses, see i have chosen bezalel son of uri, the son of hur,of the tribe of judah, and i have filled him with the spirit of god.

Moreover i have appointed oholiab son of ahisamak of the tribe of dan to help him.

Then moses would return to the camp,but his young aide joshua son of nun did not leave the tent.

Nadab,abihu, mishael, elzaphan.

These were the men appointed from the community,the leaders of their ancestral tribes . they were the heads

---

Israel by violating the ban on taking devoted things.

The son of ethan;
Azariah
The sons born to hezron were;
Jerahmeel, ram and caleb.
From ram son to hezron
Ram was the father of
Amminadab, and amminadab the father of nahshon, the leader, of the people of judah.
Nahshon was the father of salmon, salmon the father of boaz
Boaz the father of obed and obed the father of jesse .
Jesse was the father of eliab his firstborn ; the second son was abinadab ,the third shimea, the fourth nethanel the fifth raddai, the sixth ozem and the seventh david.
Their sisters were zeruiah and abigail. zeruiah and abigil. zeruiahs three sons were abishai, joab, and asahel.
Abigail was the mother of amasa whose father was jether the ishaelite.
Caleb son of hezron

the fatherjair

of the clans of israel . moses and aaron took these men whose names had been specified, and they called the whole community together on the first day of the second month. The people registered their ancestry by their clans and families, and the men twenty years old or more were listed by name one by one . as the lord commanded moses . and so he counted them in the desert of sinai.

The number from the tribe of reuben was 46,500
The number from the tribe of gad was 45,650
The number from the tribe of judah was 74,600
The number from the tribe of issachar was 54,400
The numbers from the tribe of zebulun was 57,400

From the sons of joseph

Israel by violating the ban on taking devoted things.

The son of ethan;
Azariah
The sons born to hezron were;
Jerahmeel, ram and caleb.
From ram son to hezron
Ram was the father of
Amminadab, and amminadab the father of nahshon, the leader, of the people of judah.
Nahshon was the father of salmon, salmon the father of boaz
Boaz the father of obed and obed the father of jesse .
Jesse was the father of eliab his firstborn ; the second son was abinadab ,the third shimea, the fourth nethanel the fifth raddai, the sixth ozem and the seventh david.
Their sisters were zeruiah and abigail. zeruiah and abigil. zeruiahs three sons were abishai, joab, and asahel.
Abigail was the mother of amasa whose father was jether the ishaelite.
Caleb son of hezron

the fatherjair

The number from the tribe of ephraim was 40,500

The number from the tribe of manasseh 32,200

The number from the tribe of benjamin was 35,400

The number from the tribe of dan was 62,700

The number from the tribe of asher was 41,500

The number from the tribe of naphtali was 53,400

All of the israelites twenty years old or more who were able to serve in israel's army were counted according to their families. The total number was 603,550.

Israel by violating the ban on taking devoted things.

The son of ethan;
Azariah
The sons born to hezron were;
Jerahmeel, ram and caleb.
From ram son to hezron
Ram was the father of
Amminadab, and amminadab the father of nahshon, the leader, of the people of judah.
Nahshon was the father of salmon, salmon the father of boaz
Boaz the father of obed and obed the father of jesse .
Jesse was the father of eliab his firstborn ; the second son was abinadab ,the third shimea, the fourth nethanel the fifth raddai, the sixth ozem and the seventh david.
Their sisters were zeruiah and abigail. zeruiah and abigil. zeruiahs three sons were abishai, joab, and asahel.
Abigail was the mother of amasa whose father was jether the ishaelite.
Caleb son of hezron

the fatherjair

The ancestral tribe of the levites,however was not counted alone with the other's.

The total number of the levites counted at the lord's command by moses and aaron according to their clans including every male a month old or more was 22,000

So moses counted all the firstborn of the israelites as the lord commanded him

The total number of firstborn males a month old or more listed by name was 22,273

Moses and aaron and the leaders of the community counted the kohathites counted by clans were 2,750 the

Israel by violating the ban on taking devoted things.

The son of ethan;
Azariah
The sons born to hezron were;
Jerahmeel, ram and caleb.
From ram son to hezron
Ram was the father of
Amminadab, and amminadab the father of nahshon, the leader, of the people of judah.
Nahshon was the father of salmon, salmon the father of boaz
Boaz the father of obed and obed the father of jesse .
Jesse was the father of eliab his firstborn ; the second son was abinadab ,the third shimea, the fourth nethanel the fifth raddai, the sixth ozem and the seventh david.
Their sisters were zeruiah and abigail. zeruiah and abigil. zeruiahs three sons were abishai, joab, and asahel.
Abigail was the mother of amasa whose father was jether the ishaelite.
Caleb son of hezron

the fatherjair

gershonite were counted by clans 2,630 the merarites were counted by their clans were 3,200

The one who brought his offering on the first day was nahshon son of amminadab of the tribe of judah.

On the second day nethanel son of zuar, the leader of issachar, brought his offering.

On the third day, eliab son of helon, the leader of the people of zebulun, brought his offering.

On the fourth day elizur son of shedeur, the leader of the people of feuben, brought his offering.

Israel by violating the ban on taking devoted things.

The son of ethan;
Azariah
The sons born to hezron were;
Jerahmeel, ram and caleb.
From ram son to hezron
Ram was the father of
Amminadab, and amminadab the father of nahshon, the leader, of the people of judah.
Nahshon was the father of salmon, salmon the father of boaz
Boaz the father of obed and obed the father of jesse .
Jesse was the father of eliab his firstborn ; the second son was abinadab ,the third shimea, the fourth nethanel the fifth raddai, the sixth ozem and the seventh david.
Their sisters were zeruiah and abigail. zeruiah and abigil. zeruiahs three sons were abishai, joab, and asahel.
Abigail was the mother of amasa whose father was jether the ishaelite.
Caleb son of hezron

the fatherjair

On the fifth day shelumiel son of zurishaddal, the leader of the people of simeon brought his offering.

On the sixth day eliasaph son of deuel, the leader of the people of gad, brought his offering.

On the seventh day elishama son of ammihud, the leader of the people of ephraim, brought his offering.

On the eighth day gamaliel son of pedahzur, the leader of the people of manasseh,brought his offering.

On the ninth day abidan son of gideoni, the leader of the people of benjamin, brought his offering.

Israel by violating the ban on taking devoted things.

The son of ethan;
Azariah
The sons born to hezron were;
Jerahmeel, ram and caleb.
From ram son to hezron
Ram was the father of
Amminadab, and amminadab the father of nahshon, the leader, of the people of judah.
Nahshon was the father of salmon, salmon the father of boaz
Boaz the father of obed and obed the father of jesse .
Jesse was the father of eliab his firstborn ; the second son was abinadab ,the third shimea, the fourth nethanel the fifth raddai, the sixth ozem and the seventh david.
Their sisters were zeruiah and abigail. zeruiah and abigil. zeruiahs three sons were abishai, joab, and asahel.
Abigail was the mother of amasa whose father was jether the ishaelite.
Caleb son of hezron

the fatherjair

On the tenth day ahiezer son of ammishaddai, the leader of the people of dan,brought his offering.

On the eleventh day pagiel son of okran, the leader of the people of asher, brought his offering.

On the twelfth day ahira son of enan, the leader of the people of naphtali, brought his offering.

The lord said to moses send some men to explore the land of canaan, which i am giving to the israelites, from each ancestral tribe send one of its leaders.

So the lord commanded moses sent them out from the desert of paran. All of them were leaders of the israelites, these are their names.

Israel by violating the ban on taking devoted things.

The son of ethan;
Azariah
The sons born to hezron were;
Jerahmeel, ram and caleb.
From ram son to hezron
Ram was the father of
Amminadab, and amminadab the father of nahshon, the leader, of the people of judah.
Nahshon was the father of salmon, salmon the father of boaz
Boaz the father of obed and obed the father of jesse .
Jesse was the father of eliab his firstborn ; the second son was abinadab ,the third shimea, the fourth nethanel the fifth raddai, the sixth ozem and the seventh david.
Their sisters were zeruiah and abigail. zeruiah and abigil. zeruiahs three sons were abishai, joab, and asahel.
Abigail was the mother of amasa whose father was jether the ishaelite.
Caleb son of hezron

the fatherjair

From the tribe of reuben, shammua son of zakkur; from the tribe of simeon shaphat son of hori; from the tribe of judah,caleb son of jephunneh; from the tribe of issachar, lgal son of joseph;

From the tribe of ephraim, hoshea son of nun; from the tribe of benjamin,palti son of raphu;

From the tribe of zebulun, gaddiel son of sodi; from the tribe of manasseh (a tribe of joseph)

Gaddi son of susi;

From the tribe of dan, ammiel son of gemalli; from the tribe of asher, sethur son of michael;

Israel by violating the ban on taking devoted things.

The son of ethan;
Azariah
The sons born to hezron were;
Jerahmeel, ram and caleb.
From ram son to hezron
Ram was the father of
Amminadab, and amminadab the father of nahshon, the leader, of the people of judah.
Nahshon was the father of salmon, salmon the father of boaz
Boaz the father of obed and obed the father of jesse .
Jesse was the father of eliab his firstborn ; the second son was abinadab ,the third shimea, the fourth nethanel the fifth raddai, the sixth ozem and the seventh david.
Their sisters were zeruiah and abigail. zeruiah and abigil. zeruiahs three sons were abishai, joab, and asahel.
Abigail was the mother of amasa whose father was jether the ishaelite.
Caleb son of hezron

the fatherjair

From the tribe of naphtali,nabbi son of vophsi.

From the tribe of gab,geuel son of maki.

Korah son of ishar,the son of kohath,the son of levi and certain reubenites------dathan and abiram, son's of eliab.

Balak, balaam, amalek, zimri son of salu,

These were the israelites, who came out of egypt

The descendants of reuben, the first born son of israel were,

Through hanok, the hanokite clan;

Israel by violating the ban on taking devoted things.

The son of ethan;
Azariah
The sons born to hezron were;
Jerahmeel, ram and caleb.
From ram son to hezron
Ram was the father of
Amminadab, and amminadab the father of nahshon, the leader, of the people of judah.
Nahshon was the father of salmon, salmon the father of boaz
Boaz the father of obed and obed the father of jesse .
Jesse was the father of eliab his firstborn ; the second son was abinadab ,the third shimea, the fourth nethanel the fifth raddai, the sixth ozem and the seventh david.
Their sisters were zeruiah and abigail. zeruiah and abigil. zeruiahs three sons were abishai, joab, and asahel.
Abigail was the mother of amasa whose father was jether the ishaelite.
Caleb son of hezron

the fatherjair

Through pallu, the palluite clan.

Through hezron, the hezron,the hezronite clan;

These were the clans of reuben those numbers were 43,730

The descendants of simeon by their clan were,

Through nemuel,the nemuelites

Though jamin, the jaminite clan.

Through zerah, the zerahite clan.

Though shaul,the shaulite clan.

Israel by violating the ban on taking devoted things.

The son of ethan;
Azariah
The sons born to hezron were;
Jerahmeel, ram and caleb.
From ram son to hezron
Ram was the father of
Amminadab, and amminadab the father of nahshon, the leader, of
the people of judah.
Nahshon was the father of salmon, salmon the father of boaz
Boaz the father of obed and obed the father of jesse .
Jesse was the father of eliab his firstborn ; the second son was
abinadab ,the third shimea, the fourth nethanel the fifth raddai, the
sixth ozem and the seventh david.
Their sisters were zeruiah and abigail. zeruiah and abigil. zeruiahs
three sons were abishai, joab, and asahel.
Abigail was the mother of amasa whose father was jether the ishaelite.
Caleb son of hezron

the fatherjair

These were the clans of simeon; those numbered were 22,200

These were the clans of gad;those numbered were 40,500

Er, and onan were sons of judah,but they died in canaan.

These were the clans of judah those numbered were 76,500

The clans of lssachar; those numbered were 64,300

The clans of zebulun,those numbered were 60,500

There were clans of manasseh those numbered were 52,700

Israel by violating the ban on taking devoted things.

The son of ethan;
Azariah
The sons born to hezron were;
Jerahmeel, ram and caleb.
From ram son to hezron
Ram was the father of
Amminadab, and amminadab the father of nahshon, the leader, of
the people of judah.
Nahshon was the father of salmon, salmon the father of boaz
Boaz the father of obed and obed the father of jesse .
Jesse was the father of eliab his firstborn ; the second son was
abinadab ,the third shimea, the fourth nethanel the fifth raddai, the
sixth ozem and the seventh david.
Their sisters were zeruiah and abigail. zeruiah and abigil. zeruiahs
three sons were abishai, joab, and asahel.
Abigail was the mother of amasa whose father was jether the ishaelite.
Caleb son of hezron

the fatherjair

The clan of ephraim,those numbered were 32,500

These were the clans of benjamin those numbered were 45,600

The clans of asher,those numbered were 53,400

The clans of naphtali, those numbered were 45,400

Joshua------------------samson   elimelek,   naomi, mahlon,kilion.

Orpah, ruth, boaz, obed,jesse, david, this then is the family line of perez

Perez the father of hezron,

Israel by violating the ban on taking devoted things.

The son of ethan;
Azariah
The sons born to hezron were;
Jerahmeel, ram and caleb.
From ram son to hezron
Ram was the father of
Amminadab, and amminadab the father of nahshon, the leader, of the people of judah.
Nahshon was the father of salmon, salmon the father of boaz
Boaz the father of obed and obed the father of jesse .
Jesse was the father of eliab his firstborn ; the second son was abinadab ,the third shimea, the fourth nethanel the fifth raddai, the sixth ozem and the seventh david.
Their sisters were zeruiah and abigail. zeruiah and abigil. zeruiahs three sons were abishai, joab, and asahel.
Abigail was the mother of amasa whose father was jether the ishaelite.
Caleb son of hezron

the fatherjair

Hezron the father of ram

Ram the father of amminadab

Amminadab the father of nahshon,

Nahshon the father of salmon

Salmon the father of boaz

Boaz the father of obed

Obed the father of jesse

And jesse the father of david

Israel by violating the ban on taking devoted things.

The son of ethan;
Azariah
The sons born to hezron were;
Jerahmeel, ram and caleb.
From ram son to hezron
Ram was the father of
Amminadab, and amminadab the father of nahshon, the leader, of
the people of judah.
Nahshon was the father of salmon, salmon the father of boaz
Boaz the father of obed and obed the father of jesse .
Jesse was the father of eliab his firstborn ; the second son was
abinadab ,the third shimea, the fourth nethanel the fifth raddai, the
sixth ozem and the seventh david.
Their sisters were zeruiah and abigail. zeruiah and abigil. zeruiahs
three sons were abishai, joab, and asahel.
Abigail was the mother of amasa whose father was jether the ishaelite.
Caleb son of hezron

the fatherjair

Samuel, elkanah, son of jeroham, the son of elihu, the son
of tohu, the son of zuph, hannah, peninnah, eli, eli two
sons hophni, phinehas died, eli died. Ichabod, the city got
an outbreak of tumors young and old from god because
they moved the ark of the god of israel.

Tumors and rats were the same plague that struck both
sides the rulers and them,

Ashdod, gaza, ashkelon, gath, ekron, joel,abijah, matris
clan was taken saul the son of kish was taken, nahash,
jonathan, lshvi,malki, shua, merab, michal, ahinoam
the wife of saul the daughter of ahimaaz.eliab, abinadab,
shammah, david. Abner, merab, adriel, meholah.

Michal,david's wife.

Israel by violating the ban on taking devoted things.

The son of ethan;
Azariah
The sons born to hezron were;
Jerahmeel, ram and caleb.
From ram son to hezron
Ram was the father of
Amminadab, and amminadab the father of nahshon, the leader, of
the people of judah.
Nahshon was the father of salmon, salmon the father of boaz
Boaz the father of obed and obed the father of jesse .
Jesse was the father of eliab his firstborn ; the second son was
abinadab ,the third shimea, the fourth nethanel the fifth raddai, the
sixth ozem and the seventh david.
Their sisters were zeruiah and abigail. zeruiah and abigil. zeruiahs
three sons were abishai, joab, and asahel.
Abigail was the mother of amasa whose father was jether the ishaelite.
Caleb son of hezron

the fatherjair

Abigail, ahinoam,achish,

Abner, ish-bosheth, joab, abishai, these were the sons born to david in hebron, amnon, kileab,absalom, adonijah,shephatiah, ithream.

These were the names of the children him, shammua, shobab, nathan, solomon, ibhar, elishua, nepheg, japhia, elishama, eliada, eliphelet.

The ark of the lords remained in the house of obed-edom the gittite for three -months .tamar amon were in love, with tamar and wickly wanted to have sex with his sister. He raped her.

Absalom kills amnon.

Israel by violating the ban on taking devoted things.

The son of ethan;
Azariah
The sons born to hezron were;
Jerahmeel, ram and caleb.
From ram son to hezron
Ram was the father of
Amminadab, and amminadab the father of nahshon, the leader, of the people of judah.
Nahshon was the father of salmon, salmon the father of boaz
Boaz the father of obed and obed the father of jesse .
Jesse was the father of eliab his firstborn ; the second son was abinadab ,the third shimea, the fourth nethanel the fifth raddai, the sixth ozem and the seventh david.
Their sisters were zeruiah and abigail. zeruiah and abigil. zeruiahs three sons were abishai, joab, and asahel.
Abigail was the mother of amasa whose father was jether the ishaelite.
Caleb son of hezron

the fatherjair

Rizpah, abishag, king solomon,

So king solomon ruled over all of israel and these were the chief officials

Azariah son of zadok- the priest, elihoreph and ahihal,sons of shisha ---secretaries.

Jehoshaphat son of ahilub--recorder

Benaiah son of jeholada---commander of chief.

Zadok and abiathar---priests;

Azariah son of nathan - in charge of the district governors.

Israel by violating the ban on taking devoted things.

The son of ethan;
Azariah
The sons born to hezron were;
Jerahmeel, ram and caleb.
From ram son to hezron
Ram was the father of
Amminadab, and amminadab the father of nahshon, the leader, of the people of judah.
Nahshon was the father of salmon, salmon the father of boaz
Boaz the father of obed and obed the father of jesse .
Jesse was the father of eliab his firstborn ; the second son was abinadab ,the third shimea, the fourth nethanel the fifth raddai, the sixth ozem and the seventh david.
Their sisters were zeruiah and abigail. zeruiah and abigil. zeruiahs three sons were abishai, joab, and asahel.
Abigail was the mother of amasa whose father was jether the ishaelite.
Caleb son of hezron

the fatherjair

Zubud son of nathan --a priest and adviser to the king.

Ahishar---palace administrator;

Adoniram son of adba--in charge of forced labor.

Solomon had twelve district governors over all of israel, who supplied provisions for the king and the royal household. Each one had to provide supplies for one month in the year. These are their names.

elon bethhanan;

Ben-deker -in makaz, shaalbim, beth

Israel by violating the ban on taking devoted things.

The son of ethan;
Azariah
The sons born to hezron were;
Jerahmeel, ram and caleb.
From ram son to hezron
Ram was the father of
Amminadab, and amminadab the father of nahshon, the leader, of the people of judah.
Nahshon was the father of salmon, salmon the father of boaz
Boaz the father of obed and obed the father of jesse .
Jesse was the father of eliab his firstborn ; the second son was abinadab ,the third shimea, the fourth nethanel the fifth raddai, the sixth ozem and the seventh david.
Their sisters were zeruiah and abigail. zeruiah and abigil. zeruiahs three sons were abishai, joab, and asahel.
Abigail was the mother of amasa whose father was jether the ishaelite.
Caleb son of hezron

the fatherjair

Ben–abinadad –in naphoth dor (he was married to taphath daughter of solomon);

Baana son of ahilud-----in tannach and megiddo,and all of beth-shan next to zarethan below jezzeel,from beth shan to abel meholah across to jokmeam

Ben-geber-in ramoth gilead (the settelments of jair son of manasseh in gilead were his,as well as the region of argob in bashan and its sixty large walled cities with bronze gate bars);

Ahinadad son of iddo -in mahanaim;

Ahimaaz-in naphtali (he had married basemath daughter of solomon);

Israel by violating the ban on taking devoted things.

The son of ethan;
Azariah
The sons born to hezron were;
Jerahmeel, ram and caleb.
From ram son to hezron
Ram was the father of
Amminadab, and amminadab the father of nahshon, the leader, of the people of judah.
Nahshon was the father of salmon, salmon the father of boaz
Boaz the father of obed and obed the father of jesse .
Jesse was the father of eliab his firstborn ; the second son was abinadab ,the third shimea, the fourth nethanel the fifth raddai, the sixth ozem and the seventh david.
Their sisters were zeruiah and abigail. zeruiah and abigil. zeruiahs three sons were abishai, joab, and asahel.
Abigail was the mother of amasa whose father was jether the ishaelite.
Caleb son of hezron

the fatherjair

Baana son of hushai ---in asher and in aloth

Jehoshaphat son of paruah---in issachar;

Shimei son of ela--in benjamin

Geber son of uri --- in gilead (the country of sihon king of the amorites and the country of og king of bashan) he was the only governor over the district .solomon had 700 wives as he got older his wives led him astray and turned his heart to other gods, he did the same for all his wives,who burned incense and offered sacrifices to their god.

Rehoboam king of judah son of solomon

Israel by violating the ban on taking devoted things.

The son of ethan;
Azariah
The sons born to hezron were;
Jerahmeel, ram and caleb.
From ram son to hezron
Ram was the father of
Amminadab, and amminadab the father of nahshon, the leader, of the people of judah.
Nahshon was the father of salmon, salmon the father of boaz
Boaz the father of obed and obed the father of jesse .
Jesse was the father of eliab his firstborn ; the second son was abinadab ,the third shimea, the fourth nethanel the fifth raddai, the sixth ozem and the seventh david.
Their sisters were zeruiah and abigail. zeruiah and abigil. zeruiahs three sons were abishai, joab, and asahel.
Abigail was the mother of amasa whose father was jether the ishaelite.
Caleb son of hezron

the fatherjair

Abijah his son became king of judah

Nadab king of israel

Elah king of israel

Zimri king of israel

Omri king of israel

Ahab king of israel

Elijah, elisha, naaman,jehoram, hazael

Ahaziah king of judah

Israel by violating the ban on taking devoted things.

The son of ethan;
Azariah
The sons born to hezron were;
Jerahmeel, ram and caleb.
From ram son to hezron
Ram was the father of
Amminadab, and amminadab the father of nahshon, the leader, of
the people of judah.
Nahshon was the father of salmon, salmon the father of boaz
Boaz the father of obed and obed the father of jesse .
Jesse was the father of eliab his firstborn ; the second son was
abinadab ,the third shimea, the fourth nethanel the fifth raddai, the
sixth ozem and the seventh david.
Their sisters were zeruiah and abigail. zeruiah and abigil. zeruiahs
three sons were abishai, joab, and asahel.
Abigail was the mother of amasa whose father was jether the ishaelite.
Caleb son of hezron

the fatherjair

Jehu anointed king of israel

Jehoahaz king of israel

Jehoash king of israel

Amaziah king of judah

Zechariah king of israel

Shallum king of israel

Menahem king of israel

Pekahiah king of israel

Israel by violating the ban on taking devoted things.

The son of ethan;
Azariah
The sons born to hezron were;
Jerahmeel, ram and caleb.
From ram son to hezron
Ram was the father of
Amminadab, and amminadab the father of nahshon, the leader, of
the people of judah.
Nahshon was the father of salmon, salmon the father of boaz
Boaz the father of obed and obed the father of jesse .
Jesse was the father of eliab his firstborn ; the second son was
abinadab ,the third shimea, the fourth nethanel the fifth raddai, the
sixth ozem and the seventh david.
Their sisters were zeruiah and abigail. zeruiah and abigil. zeruiahs
three sons were abishai, joab, and asahel.
Abigail was the mother of amasa whose father was jether the ishaelite.
Caleb son of hezron

the fatherjair

Pekah king of israel

Jotham the king of judah

Ahaz king of judah

Hoshea last king of israel

Israel exiled because of sin the israelites had sin against the lord their god who brought them up out of egypt from under the power of pharaoh king of egypt, they worship other gods.and followed the practices of nations the lord had driven out before them as well as the practices that the king of israel had introduce, the israelites secretly did things against the lord their god .hezekiah, isaiah,

---

Israel by violating the ban on taking devoted things.

The son of ethan;
Azariah
The sons born to hezron were;
Jerahmeel, ram and caleb.
From ram son to hezron
Ram was the father of
Amminadab, and amminadab the father of nahshon, the leader, of
the people of judah.
Nahshon was the father of salmon, salmon the father of boaz
Boaz the father of obed and obed the father of jesse .
Jesse was the father of eliab his firstborn ; the second son was
abinadab ,the third shimea, the fourth nethanel the fifth raddai, the
sixth ozem and the seventh david.
Their sisters were zeruiah and abigail. zeruiah and abigil. zeruiahs
three sons were abishai, joab, and asahel.
Abigail was the mother of amasa whose father was jether the ishaelite.
Caleb son of hezron

the fatherjair

Historical records from adam to abraham to noah's sons

Adam,seth,enosh,kenan,mahalalel,jared,enoch,
methuselah, lamech, noah.

The son's of noah.;

Shem, ham, japheth.

The japdanithites;

The sons of japheth;

Gomer, magog, madai, javan, tubal, meshek, and tiras.

The sons of gomer;

Israel by violating the ban on taking devoted things.

The son of ethan;
Azariah
The sons born to hezron were;
Jerahmeel, ram and caleb.
From ram son to hezron
Ram was the father of
Amminadab, and amminadab the father of nahshon, the leader, of
the people of judah.
Nahshon was the father of salmon, salmon the father of boaz
Boaz the father of obed and obed the father of jesse .
Jesse was the father of eliab his firstborn ; the second son was
abinadab ,the third shimea, the fourth nethanel the fifth raddai, the
sixth ozem and the seventh david.
Their sisters were zeruiah and abigail. zeruiah and abigil. zeruiahs
three sons were abishai, joab, and asahel.
Abigail was the mother of amasa whose father was jether the ishaelite.
Caleb son of hezron

the fatherjair

Ashkenaz, riphath, and togarmah.

The sons of javan;

Elishah, tarshish, the kittites, and rodanites.

The hamites;

The sons of ham

Cush, egypt, put and canaan.

The sons of cush;

Seba, havilah, sabta, raamah,and sabteka.

Israel by violating the ban on taking devoted things.

The son of ethan;
Azariah
The sons born to hezron were;
Jerahmeel, ram and caleb.
From ram son to hezron
Ram was the father of
Amminadab, and amminadab the father of nahshon, the leader, of
the people of judah.
Nahshon was the father of salmon, salmon the father of boaz
Boaz the father of obed and obed the father of jesse .
Jesse was the father of eliab his firstborn ; the second son was
abinadab ,the third shimea, the fourth nethanel the fifth raddai, the
sixth ozem and the seventh david.
Their sisters were zeruiah and abigail. zeruiah and abigil. zeruiahs
three sons were abishai, joab, and asahel.
Abigail was the mother of amasa whose father was jether the ishaelite.
Caleb son of hezron

the fatherjair

The sons of raamah;

Sheba and dedan;

Cush was the father of

Nimrod, who became a mighty warrior on earth.

Egypt was the father of the ludites, anamites, lehabites,naphtuhites, pathrusites, kasluhites,(from whom the philistines came) and caphtorites,

Canaan was the father

Israel by violating the ban on taking devoted things.

The son of ethan;
Azariah
The sons born to hezron were;
Jerahmeel, ram and caleb.
From ram son to hezron
Ram was the father of
Amminadab, and amminadab the father of nahshon, the leader, of the people of judah.
Nahshon was the father of salmon, salmon the father of boaz
Boaz the father of obed and obed the father of jesse .
Jesse was the father of eliab his firstborn ; the second son was abinadab ,the third shimea, the fourth nethanel the fifth raddai, the sixth ozem and the seventh david.
Their sisters were zeruiah and abigail. zeruiah and abigil. zeruiahs three sons were abishai, joab, and asahel.
Abigail was the mother of amasa whose father was jether the ishaelite.
Caleb son of hezron

the fatherjair

Sidon his firstborn,and of the hittites,jebusites,amorites, girgashites, hivites,arkites, sinites,arvadites, zemarites and hamathites . the semites, the sons of sem

Elam, ashur, arphaxad, lud, and abram;

Uz,hul, gether, and meshek.

Arphaxad was the father of shelah,

And shelah the father of eber.

Two sons were born to eber;

One was named peleg, because in his time the earth was divided, his brother was named joktan.

Israel by violating the ban on taking devoted things.

The son of ethan;
Azariah
The sons born to hezron were;
Jerahmeel, ram and caleb.
From ram son to hezron
Ram was the father of
Amminadab, and amminadab the father of nahshon, the leader, of the people of judah.
Nahshon was the father of salmon, salmon the father of boaz
Boaz the father of obed and obed the father of jesse .
Jesse was the father of eliab his firstborn ; the second son was abinadab ,the third shimea, the fourth nethanel the fifth raddai, the sixth ozem and the seventh david.
Their sisters were zeruiah and abigail. zeruiah and abigil. zeruiahs three sons were abishai, joab, and asahel.
Abigail was the mother of amasa whose father was jether the ishaelite.
Caleb son of hezron

the fatherjair

Joktan was the father of, almodad, sheleph, hazarmaveth, jerah,hadoram, uzal, diklah. Obal, abimael,sheba,ophir, havilah and jobad. All these were sons of joktan.

Shem,arphaxad, shelah,

Eber,peleg, reu,

Serug, nahor, terah, and abram(that is,abraham)

The family of abraham

The sons of abraham;

Isaac and ishmael;

Israel by violating the ban on taking devoted things.

The son of ethan;
Azariah
The sons born to hezron were;
Jerahmeel, ram and caleb.
From ram son to hezron
Ram was the father of
Amminadab, and amminadab the father of nahshon, the leader, of the people of judah.
Nahshon was the father of salmon, salmon the father of boaz
Boaz the father of obed and obed the father of jesse .
Jesse was the father of eliab his firstborn ; the second son was abinadab ,the third shimea, the fourth nethanel the fifth raddai, the sixth ozem and the seventh david.
Their sisters were zeruiah and abigail. zeruiah and abigil. zeruiahs three sons were abishai, joab, and asahel.
Abigail was the mother of amasa whose father was jether the ishaelite.
Caleb son of hezron

the fatherjair

Descendants of hager

These were their descendants;

Nebaioth,the firstborn of ismael,kedar, adbeel, mibsam, mishma,dumah, massa, hadad, tema, jetur,naphish, and kedemah. These were the sons of ishmael.

Descendants of keturah

The sons born to keturah abraham's concubine; zimran,jokshan, medan, midian, ishbak and shuah.

The sons of jokshan;

Sheba and dedan.

Israel by violating the ban on taking devoted things.

The son of ethan;
Azariah
The sons born to hezron were;
Jerahmeel, ram and caleb.
From ram son to hezron
Ram was the father of
Amminadab, and amminadab the father of nahshon, the leader, of the people of judah.
Nahshon was the father of salmon, salmon the father of boaz
Boaz the father of obed and obed the father of jesse .
Jesse was the father of eliab his firstborn ; the second son was abinadab ,the third shimea, the fourth nethanel the fifth raddai, the sixth ozem and the seventh david.
Their sisters were zeruiah and abigail. zeruiah and abigil. zeruiahs three sons were abishai, joab, and asahel.
Abigail was the mother of amasa whose father was jether the ishaelite.
Caleb son of hezron

the fatherjair

The sons of midian

Ephah, epher, hanok, abida and eldaah.

All these were descendants of keturah.

Descendants of sarah.

Abraham was the father of isaac.

The sons of isaac

Esau and israel.

Esau's sons

Israel by violating the ban on taking devoted things.

The son of ethan;
Azariah
The sons born to hezron were;
Jerahmeel, ram and caleb.
From ram son to hezron
Ram was the father of
Amminadab, and amminadab the father of nahshon, the leader, of
the people of judah.
Nahshon was the father of salmon, salmon the father of boaz
Boaz the father of obed and obed the father of jesse .
Jesse was the father of eliab his firstborn ; the second son was
abinadab ,the third shimea, the fourth nethanel the fifth raddai, the
sixth ozem and the seventh david.
Their sisters were zeruiah and abigail. zeruiah and abigil. zeruiahs
three sons were abishai, joab, and asahel.
Abigail was the mother of amasa whose father was jether the ishaelite.
Caleb son of hezron

the fatherjair

The sons of esau;

Eliphaz, reuel, jeush, jalam, and korah.

The son's of eliphaz;

Teman, omar, zepho, gatam, and kenaz;

By timna; amalek.

The sons of reuel;

Nahtah, zerah, shammah, and mizzah,

The people of seir in edom

Israel by violating the ban on taking devoted things.

The son of ethan;
Azariah
The sons born to hezron were;
Jerahmeel, ram and caleb.
From ram son to hezron
Ram was the father of
Amminadab, and amminadab the father of nahshon, the leader, of the people of judah.
Nahshon was the father of salmon, salmon the father of boaz
Boaz the father of obed and obed the father of jesse .
Jesse was the father of eliab his firstborn ; the second son was abinadab ,the third shimea, the fourth nethanel the fifth raddai, the sixth ozem and the seventh david.
Their sisters were zeruiah and abigail. zeruiah and abigil. zeruiahs three sons were abishai, joab, and asahel.
Abigail was the mother of amasa whose father was jether the ishaelite.
Caleb son of hezron

the fatherjair

The sons of seir

Lotan, shobal, zibeon, anah, dishon, ezer and dishan.

The sons of lotan;

Tima was lotan's sister

Hori, and homam.

The sons of shobal;

Alvan, manahath, ebal, shepho and onam.

The sons of zibeon;

Israel by violating the ban on taking devoted things.

The son of ethan;
Azariah
The sons born to hezron were;
Jerahmeel, ram and caleb.
From ram son to hezron
Ram was the father of
Amminadab, and amminadab the father of nahshon, the leader, of
the people of judah.
Nahshon was the father of salmon, salmon the father of boaz
Boaz the father of obed and obed the father of jesse .
Jesse was the father of eliab his firstborn ; the second son was
abinadab ,the third shimea, the fourth nethanel the fifth raddai, the
sixth ozem and the seventh david.
Their sisters were zeruiah and abigail. zeruiah and abigil. zeruiahs
three sons were abishai, joab, and asahel.
Abigail was the mother of amasa whose father was jether the ishaelite.
Caleb son of hezron

the fatherjair

Alah, and anah.

The sons of anah;

Dishon.

The sons of dishon.

Hemdan, eshban, ithran and keran.

The sons of ezer;

Bihan, zaavan and akan.

The sons of dishan;

Israel by violating the ban on taking devoted things.

The son of ethan;
Azariah
The sons born to hezron were;
Jerahmeel, ram and caleb.
From ram son to hezron
Ram was the father of
Amminadab, and amminadab the father of nahshon, the leader, of the people of judah.
Nahshon was the father of salmon, salmon the father of boaz
Boaz the father of obed and obed the father of jesse .
Jesse was the father of eliab his firstborn ; the second son was abinadab ,the third shimea, the fourth nethanel the fifth raddai, the sixth ozem and the seventh david.
Their sisters were zeruiah and abigail. zeruiah and abigil. zeruiahs three sons were abishai, joab, and asahel.
Abigail was the mother of amasa whose father was jether the ishaelite. Caleb son of hezron

the fatherjair

Uz and aran.

The rulers of edom

Israel's sons

Reuben, simeon, levi, judah, issachar, zebulun, dan, joseph, benjamin, naphtali, gad and asher.

Judah

To hezons sons

The sons of judah;

Israel by violating the ban on taking devoted things.

The son of ethan;
Azariah
The sons born to hezron were;
Jerahmeel, ram and caleb.
From ram son to hezron
Ram was the father of
Amminadab, and amminadab the father of nahshon, the leader, of the people of judah.
Nahshon was the father of salmon, salmon the father of boaz
Boaz the father of obed and obed the father of jesse .
Jesse was the father of eliab his firstborn ; the second son was abinadab ,the third shimea, the fourth nethanel the fifth raddai, the sixth ozem and the seventh david.
Their sisters were zeruiah and abigail. zeruiah and abigil. zeruiahs three sons were abishai, joab, and asahel.
Abigail was the mother of amasa whose father was jether the ishaelite.
Caleb son of hezron

the fatherjair

Er, onan and shelah, these three were born to him by canaanite woman, the daughter of shua, er,judah 's firstborn,was wicket in the sight of the lord's sight; so the lord put him to death, judah's daughter-in-law tamar bore perez and zerah to judah . he had five sons in all.

The sons of perez

Hezron and hamul.

The sons of zerah;

Zimri,ethan,heman, kalkol and darda'-five in all.

The sons of karmi;

Israel by violating the ban on taking devoted things.

The son of ethan;
Azariah
The sons born to hezron were;
Jerahmeel, ram and caleb.
From ram son to hezron
Ram was the father of
Amminadab, and amminadab the father of nahshon, the leader, of the people of judah.
Nahshon was the father of salmon, salmon the father of boaz
Boaz the father of obed and obed the father of jesse .
Jesse was the father of eliab his firstborn ; the second son was abinadab ,the third shimea, the fourth nethanel the fifth raddai, the sixth ozem and the seventh david.
Their sisters were zeruiah and abigail. zeruiah and abigil. zeruiahs three sons were abishai, joab, and asahel.
Abigail was the mother of amasa whose father was jether the ishaelite.
Caleb son of hezron

the fatherjair

Achar, who brought trouble on is

These were the son's of david born to him in hebron

The firstborn was amnon the son of ahinoam of jezreel;

The second,daniel the son of abigail of carmel;

The third,absalom the son of maakah daughter of talmi king of geshur;

The fourth adonijah the son of haggith;

The fifth,sephatiah the son of abital;

And the sixth, ithream,by his wife eglah;

Israel by violating the ban on taking devoted things.

The son of ethan;
Azariah
The sons born to hezron were;
Jerahmeel, ram and caleb.
From ram son to hezron
Ram was the father of
Amminadab, and amminadab the father of nahshon, the leader, of the people of judah.
Nahshon was the father of salmon, salmon the father of boaz
Boaz the father of obed and obed the father of jesse .
Jesse was the father of eliab his firstborn ; the second son was abinadab ,the third shimea, the fourth nethanel the fifth raddai, the sixth ozem and the seventh david.
Their sisters were zeruiah and abigail. zeruiah and abigil. zeruiahs three sons were abishai, joab, and asahel.
Abigail was the mother of amasa whose father was jether the ishaelite.
Caleb son of hezron

the fatherjair

These six were born to david in hebron, where he reigned seven years and six months

David reigned in jerusalem thirty -three years and these were the children born to him there.

Shammua, shobab,nathan, and solomon.

These were the four were by bathsheba daughter of ammiel,

Israel by violating the ban on taking devoted things.

The son of ethan;
Azariah
The sons born to hezron were;
Jerahmeel, ram and caleb.
From ram son to hezron
Ram was the father of
Amminadab, and amminadab the father of nahshon, the leader, of the people of judah.
Nahshon was the father of salmon, salmon the father of boaz
Boaz the father of obed and obed the father of jesse .
Jesse was the father of eliab his firstborn ; the second son was abinadab ,the third shimea, the fourth nethanel the fifth raddai, the sixth ozem and the seventh david.
Their sisters were zeruiah and abigail. zeruiah and abigil. zeruiahs three sons were abishai, joab, and asahel.
Abigail was the mother of amasa whose father was jether the ishaelite.
Caleb son of hezron

the fatherjair

Job, isaiah, matthew, jesus, mark, luke,john, peter, timothy, paul,moses,archangel michael.

The 12 apostles and disciples simon, andrew,james,john, philip,bartholomew, matthew,thomas,james the son of alphaeus,judas son of james,and judas iscariot,who became a traitor. mary

Rachal,john the baptist thaddaeus, hailmary, arron,

Israel by violating the ban on taking devoted things.

The son of ethan;
Azariah
The sons born to hezron were;
Jerahmeel, ram and caleb.
From ram son to hezron
Ram was the father of
Amminadab, and amminadab the father of nahshon, the leader, of the people of judah.
Nahshon was the father of salmon, salmon the father of boaz
Boaz the father of obed and obed the father of jesse .
Jesse was the father of eliab his firstborn ; the second son was abinadab ,the third shimea, the fourth nethanel the fifth raddai, the sixth ozem and the seventh david.
Their sisters were zeruiah and abigail. zeruiah and abigil. zeruiahs three sons were abishai, joab, and asahel.
Abigail was the mother of amasa whose father was jether the ishaelite.
Caleb son of hezron

the fatherjair

The father of jair,who controlled twenty three towns
in gilead, (but geshur and aram captured havvoth jair;
Jerahmeel son of hezron
ram his firstborn,bunah, oren, ozem and
ahijah, jerahmeel had another wife,whose name
was atarah; she was the mother of onam

Israel by violating the ban on taking devoted things.

The son of ethan;
Azariah
The sons born to hezron were;
Jerahmeel, ram and caleb.
From ram son to hezron
Ram was the father of
Amminadab, and amminadab the father of nahshon, the leader, of
the people of judah.
Nahshon was the father of salmon, salmon the father of boaz
Boaz the father of obed and obed the father of jesse .
Jesse was the father of eliab his firstborn ; the second son was
abinadab ,the third shimea, the fourth nethanel the fifth raddai, the
sixth ozem and the seventh david.
Their sisters were zeruiah and abigail. zeruiah and abigil. zeruiahs
three sons were abishai, joab, and asahel.
Abigail was the mother of amasa whose father was jether the ishaelite.
Caleb son of hezron

the fatherjair

Matthan the father of jacob,and jacob the father of joseph,the husband of mary, and mary the mother of jesus who is called the messiah. Thus were fourteen generations in all from abraham to david, fourteen from david to the exile to babylon and fourteen from exile to the messiah.

This is how the birth of jesus the messiah came about,his mother mary was pledged to be married to joseph,but before they came together,she was found to be pregnant through the Holy spirit. because Joseph her husband was faithful to the law,and yet did not want to expose to the public disgrace,disgrace he had in mind to divorce her quietly.

Israel by violating the ban on taking devoted things.

The son of ethan;
Azariah
The sons born to hezron were;
Jerahmeel, ram and caleb.
From ram son to hezron
Ram was the father of
Amminadab, and amminadab the father of nahshon, the leader, of the people of judah.
Nahshon was the father of salmon, salmon the father of boaz
Boaz the father of obed and obed the father of jesse .
Jesse was the father of eliab his firstborn ; the second son was abinadab ,the third shimea, the fourth nethanel the fifth raddai, the sixth ozem and the seventh david.
Their sisters were zeruiah and abigail. zeruiah and abigil. zeruiahs three sons were abishai, joab, and asahel.
Abigail was the mother of amasa whose father was jether the ishaelite.
Caleb son of hezron

the fatherjair

Printed in the United States
By Bookmasters